# THE ULTIMATE
# Bible Quiz Book

## Douglas A. Jacoby

HARVEST HOUSE PUBLISHERS

EUGENE, OREGON

Cover by Dugan Design Group, Bloomington, Minnesota

Cover illustration © iStockphoto/Tomacco

**THE ULTIMATE BIBLE QUIZ BOOK**
Copyright © 2008 by Douglas A. Jacoby
Published by Harvest House Publishers
Eugene, Oregon 97402
www.harvesthousepublishers.com

ISBN 978-0-7369-3051-2

**Printed in the United States of America**

11 12 13 14 15 16 17 18 19 / VP-SK / 10 9 8 7 6 5 4 3 2

# Contents

# Foreword

## Why a Quiz Book?

Why do we need a Bible quiz book? Isn't head knowledge without heart knowledge a dangerous combination?

Of course it is (1 Corinthians 8:1). But why should the quest for knowledge be at odds with the goal to love the Lord our God with all our hearts? Does this have to be an either-or choice?

As Jesus relates the greatest commandment (Deuteronomy 6:5), he brings out its deeper meaning. In Matthew 22:37, Mark 12:30, and Luke 10:27, he adds *mind* to the equation. We are to love God with all our heart, soul, strength, and mind. Well, are we doing that—loving God with all our mind?

### Mathetai

Christians often shrink from the intellectual side of the faith for various reasons. ("I'm too busy to read…I have trouble concentrating…I think prayer is more important.") But surely this is to deny our Master his right to be Lord of all, including our minds. Let's think about the word often used in the book of Acts for Christians: *disciples.* In fact, the Bible uses many names for a follower of Jesus Christ. *Believer, brother, saint, Christian,* and *disciple* are the most common ones. Each term emphasizes a different aspect of our common experience or attitude in Christ. The word translated *disciple* in the Greek New Testament is *mathetes* (mah-they-tays). What does this mean? *Mathetes* comes from the verb *manthanein,* which means "to learn." Thus, *mathetai* (plural) are learners. The lexicon defines *disciple* as "learner, student, pupil, apprentice," so all these meanings are reasonable translations.

Are we learners? Some Christians think they're too old to be learners or students. And yet we see in God's Word that if we aren't learners, we aren't really followers of Jesus Christ. Each one of us is called, regardless of age, gender, education, or culture, to be a student. We are to be students of human nature and the world around us, persons eager to learn from anything and anyone. Above all, we are called to be avid students of the Word. Am I accurately described as a student? This isn't the only aspect of biblical Christianity that should be stressed—I hope I am also a true believer, a loyal brother, and a devoted saint with a thoroughly Christian mind-set—but it is certainly a fundamental one. Being learners means that we must ask questions. It also entails being questioned and defending our faith.

Testing proves character. Tests solidify knowledge. Although not in an academic context, in 2 Corinthians 13:5 Paul tells his readers, "Test yourselves." (Some versions read "Examine yourselves.") To cement knowledge into our memory so that it doesn't slip away, there is nothing like a good test!

I put together *The Ultimate Bible Quiz Book* with this in mind. It contains 109 Bible quizzes for your learning and enjoyment. Some are only a few questions long, while the longest, "The Cosmic Bible Quiz," contains 100. Questions come from all 66 books of the Bible. I've even included a time test so you can see how fast you are!

May the Lord use this little book to sharpen our minds, whet our spiritual appetites, and draw us closer to Him.

Test yourself!

Douglas Jacoby
Marietta, Georgia

# Jesus, Paul, and Peter

## Bible Quiz 1: About Jesus Christ

1. Jesus was Jewish. True or false?

2. What is the incarnation of Christ?

3. When did the ascension of Christ take place?

4. What is the accession of Christ?

5. Does the Bible give us any description of the physical appearance of Christ?

6. The earliest prophecy of the Messiah appears in which Old Testament book?

7. Jesus never wrote a book. True or false?

8. Jesus is mentioned by name in every book of the New Testament. True or false?

9. In which town was Jesus born?

10. Match the following words for Jesus with their respective languages:

    Gesu        German

    Yesus       Polish

    Jezus       Italian

    Jesús       Indonesian

    Jesus       Spanish

# Answers to Bible Quiz 1: About Jesus Christ

1. Jesus was Jewish.  **True**

2. What is the incarnation of Christ?

    **The "enfleshment" of God. God became a man (John 1:14)!**

3. When did the ascension of Christ take place?

    **Ten days before Pentecost and 40 days after the resurrection. See Luke 24 and Acts 1.**

4. What is the accession of Christ?

    **His sitting down on the throne at the right hand of God.**

5. Does the Bible give us any description of the physical appearance of Christ?

    **No, but Isaiah does refer to his battered appearance after he was physically abused.**

6. The earliest prophecy of the Messiah appears in which Old Testament book?

    **Genesis. See chapters 3; 24; and 49.**

7. Jesus never wrote a book.  **True**

8. Jesus is mentioned by name in every book of the New Testament.

    **False. He isn't mentioned by name in 3 John.**

9. In which town was Jesus born?  **Bethlehem**

10. Match the following words for Jesus with their respective languages:

    **Gesu—Italian**
    **Yesus—Indonesian**
    **Jezus—Polish**
    **Jesus—German**
    **Jesús—Spanish**

# Bible Quiz 2: About the Apostle Paul

1. What city was Saul from?

2. How many letters did Paul write to individuals?

3. Paul was a Roman citizen. True or false?

4. From what city did Paul escape in a basket?

5. How many chapters are included in the Corinthian letters (in all)?

6. How many times was Paul shipwrecked (the minimum number)?

7. Which of the following is the Spanish word for Paul: Paulo, Pawel, Pablo, or Papa?

8. Paul had only one eye. True or false?

9. Peter and Paul had a disagreement from which they never recovered. True or false?

10. Paul was the leader of the universal church in the first century. True or false?

# Answers to Bible Quiz 2: About the Apostle Paul

1. What city was Saul from?

   **Tarsus**

2. How many letters did Paul write to individuals?

   **Four: 1 and 2 Timothy; Titus; and Philemon**

3. Paul was a Roman citizen.

   **True**

4. From what city did Paul escape in a basket?

   **Damascus**

5. How many chapters are included in the Corinthian letters (in all)?

   **29**

6. How many times was Paul shipwrecked (the minimum number)?

   **Four. See 2 Corinthians 11:25 and Acts 27.**

7. Which of the following is the Spanish word for Paul?

   **Pablo**

8. Paul had only one eye.

   **False**

9. Peter and Paul had a disagreement from which they never recovered.

   **False. Compare Galatians 2:11 and 2 Peter 3:15.**

10. Paul was the leader of the universal church in the first century.

    **False. In the first century, the church had no single human leader. Both Peter and Paul had considerable influence, but neither was subordinate to the other.**

# Bible Quiz 3: About the Apostle Peter

1. Which relative of Peter did Jesus heal?

2. What was Peter's other name (his Jewish name)?

3. How many letters did the apostle Peter write?

4. How many times is Peter mentioned in the Bible: 7, 57, 157, or 1057?

5. Peter never truly walked on water. True or false?

6. What was Peter's father's name?

7. Who was Peter's younger brother?

8. What fishing village did Peter come from?

9. Cephas (Kepha) is another of his names. True or false?

10. In Greek, *Peter* means "rock." True or false?

# Answers to Bible Quiz 3: About the Apostle Peter

1. Which relative of Peter did Jesus heal?

   **His mother-in-law**

2. What was Peter's other name (his Jewish name)?

   **Simon or Simeon**

3. How many letters did the apostle Peter write?

   **Two**

4. How many times is Peter mentioned in the Bible?

   **157**

5. Peter never truly walked on water.

   **False**

6. What was Peter's father's name?

   **Jonah or Jonas or John**

7. Who was Peter's younger brother?

   **Andrew**

8. What fishing village did Peter come from?

   **Bethsaida**

9. Cephas (Kepha) is another of Peter's names.

   **True**

10. In Greek, *Peter* means "rock."

    **True**

# A to Z

## Bible Quiz 4: The A List

*(All answers begin with the letter a.)*

1. What is another name for the book of Revelation?

2. What are the extra books in the Catholic and Orthodox Old Testament called?

3. Which sons of David conspired to become king?

4. Who has been called the fastest man in the Bible? (Hint: See Genesis 2.)

5. Who was the husband of Prisca (Priscilla)?

6. Who pretended to be more sacrificial in his giving than he really was?

7. Who was initially terrified at the prospect of sharing the gospel with Saul of Tarsus?

8. Which two books of the Bible have names that start with the letter *A*?

9. Jesus Christ is presented in Scripture as the _____ and the Omega.

10. Who is responsible for writing at least 12 of the psalms?

# Answers to Bible Quiz 4: The A List

1. What is another name for the book of Revelation?

    **The Apocalypse**

2. What are the extra books in the Catholic and Orthodox Old Testament called?

    **The Apocrypha**

3. Which sons of David conspired to become king?

    **Absalom and Adonijah**

4. Who has been called the fastest man in the Bible?

    **Adam. He was first in the human race!**

5. Who was the husband of Prisca (Priscilla)?

    **Aquila**

6. Who pretended to be more sacrificial in his giving than he really was?

    **Ananias (along with his wife, Sapphira). See Acts 5.**

7. Who was initially terrified at the prospect of sharing the gospel with Saul of Tarsus?

    **Ananias. See Acts 9—this Ananias is different from the one in Acts 5.**

8. Which two books of the Bible have names that start with the letter *A*?

    **Amos and Acts**

9. Jesus Christ is presented in Scripture as the _____ and the Omega.

    **Alpha**

10. Who is responsible for writing at least 12 of the psalms?

    **Asaph**

# Bible Quiz 5: The B List

1. Who was the encouraging brother who introduced Saul (Paul) to the Jerusalem apostles?

2. Matthew 22 and Luke 14 both contain parables about a _____.

3. David, in his youth, killed the lion and the_____.

4. What was the name of the notorious prisoner released at Passover instead of Jesus?

5. Which Old Testament city (the city from which Nebuchadnezzar ruled his empire) became a symbol of the world in the book of Revelation?

6. Who was the wife of Uriah the Hittite and later became the mother of Solomon?

7. Name an apostle whose name starts with *B*.

8. Some people, instead of worshipping the God of the Bible, worship the Bible instead. What is the technical name for this mistake?

9. Who was Jeremiah's secretary? (Archaeologists identified his seal just a few years ago!)

10. How many books of the Bible have names that begin with *B*?

# Answers to Bible Quiz 5: The B List

1. Who was the encouraging brother who introduced Saul (Paul) to the Jerusalem apostles?   **Barnabas**

2. Matthew 22 and Luke 14 both contain parables about a_____.
   **Banquet**

3. David, in his youth, killed the lion and the_____.
   **Bear**

4. What was the name of the notorious prisoner released at Passover instead of Jesus?
   **Barabbas**

5. Which Old Testament city (the city from which Nebuchadnezzar ruled his empire) became a symbol of the world in the book of Revelation?
   **Babylon**

6. Who was the wife of Uriah the Hittite and later became the mother of Solomon?
   **Bathsheba**

7. Name an apostle whose name starts with *B*.   **Bartholomew**

8. Some people, instead of worshipping the God of the Bible, worship the Bible instead. What is the technical name for this mistake?
   **Bibliolatry**

9. Who was Jeremiah's secretary? (Archaeologists identified his seal just a few years ago!)   **Baruch**

10. How many books of the Bible have names that begin with *B*?
    **None**

# Bible Quiz 6: The C List

1. Where did Jesus reside after Nazareth?

2. What title did Roman emperors take in New Testament times?

3. Who, in his eighties, was just as vigorous and passionate to serve God as he had been when he first entered the Promised Land as a young man?

4. What is another name for the Promised Land?

5. Who was Ham's son (Noah's grandson)?

6. How many books of the Bible have names that begin with *C*?

7. Who was the high priest when Jesus was crucified?

8. Where was Barnabas from?

9. Name one unclean food from Leviticus 11.

10. Who had Paul left his cloak with at Troy (Troas)?

# Answers to Bible Quiz 6: The C List

1. Where did Jesus reside after Nazareth?

   **Capernaum**

2. What title did Roman emperors take in New Testament times?

   **Caesar**

3. Who, in his eighties, was just as vigorous and passionate to serve God as he had been when he first entered the Promised Land as a young man?

   **Caleb**

4. What is another name for the Promised Land?

   **Canaan**

5. Who was Ham's son (Noah's grandson)?

   **Canaan**

6. How many books of the Bible have names that begin with *C*?

   **Five: 1 and 2 Chronicles, 1 and 2 Corinthians, and Colossians**

7. Who was the high priest when Jesus was crucified?

   **Caiaphas**

8. Where was Barnabas from?

   **Cyprus**

9. Name one unclean food from Leviticus 11.

   **Camel. Perhaps you can find others!**

10. Who had Paul left his cloak with at Troy (Troas)?

    **Carpus. See 2 Timothy 4:13.**

# Bible Quiz 7: The D List

1. How many books of the Old Testament have names that begin with *D*?

2. How many books of the New Testament have names that begin with *D*?

3. What was the name of the Philistine corn god?

4. Who turned Samson over to the Philistines by arranging for him to have a haircut?

5. What body of water is approximately 1300 feet below sea level at its surface?

6. What is another name for the Ten Commandments?

7. Who led Israel in Judges 4–5?

8. Which of Paul's companions deserted the faith because "he loved this present world"?

9. Who was the "good guy" in 3 John?

10. Who was the "bad guy" in 3 John?

# Answers to Bible Quiz 7: The D List

1. How many books of the Old Testament have names that begin with *D*?

   **Two: Deuteronomy and Daniel**

2. How many books of the New Testament have names that begin with *D*?

   **None**

3. What was the name of the Philistine corn god?

   **Dagon**

4. Who turned Samson over to the Philistines by arranging for him to have a haircut?

   **Delilah**

5. What body of water is approximately 1300 feet below sea level at its surface?

   **The Dead Sea**

6. What is another name for the Ten Commandments?

   **The Decalogue, from the Greek word for "ten words"**

7. Who led Israel in Judges 4–5?

   **Deborah**

8. Which of Paul's companions deserted the faith because "he loved this present world"?

   **Demas**

9. Who was the "good guy" in 3 John?

   **Demetrius**

10. Who was the "bad guy" in 3 John?

    **Diotrephes**

# Bible Quiz 8: The E List

1. How many books of the Old Testament have names that begin with *E*?

2. How many books of the New Testament have names that begin with *E*?

3. Which famous garden appears early in the Bible?

4. Which nation became a biblical symbol for slavery and oppression?

5. Who miraculously fed 100 people?

6. Who planted the church at Colosse?

7. Who was apparently the first to be baptized in the province of Asia?

8. What was the common Old Testament word for God (in Hebrew)?

9. Who worked alongside Nehemiah and devoted himself to the study and observance of the Law?

10. Who was the city treasurer at Corinth?

# Answers to Bible Quiz 8: The E List

1. How many books of the Old Testament have names that begin with *E*?

   **Five: Exodus, Ezra, Esther, Ecclesiastes, and Ezekiel**

2. How many books of the New Testament have names that begin with *E*?

   **One: Ephesians**

3. Which famous garden appears early in the Bible?

   **Eden**

4. Which nation became a biblical symbol for slavery and oppression?

   **Egypt**

5. Who miraculously fed 100 people?

   **Elisha. Not quite as stunning as Jesus' miracles, is it?**

6. Who planted the church at Colosse?

   **Epaphras**

7. Who was apparently the first to be baptized in the province of Asia?

   **Epenetus. See Romans 16:5.**

8. What was the common Old Testament Hebrew word for God?

   **Elohim (also El and Elim)**

9. Who worked alongside Nehemiah and devoted himself to the study and observance of the Law?

   **Ezra**

10. Who was the city treasurer at Corinth?

    **Erastus. See Acts 19:22; Romans 16:23; 2 Timothy 4:20.**

# Bible Quiz 9: The F List

1. In the book of Genesis, what did Joseph predict would impoverish his world?

2. In the book of Acts, what did Agabus predict would hit the Roman world hard?

3. Who preferred to send for Paul at his own convenience?

4. "They devoted themselves to the apostles' teaching and to the _____."

5. In Mark 1:16-20, what did Jesus promise his disciples they would become?

6. How many years did David reign as king?

7. What word in older English Bibles refers to premarital sex?

8. In a parable in Luke, the rich _____ was told he would forfeit his life that very night.

9. In Galatians 5, we read about nine characteristics of the _____ of the Spirit.

10. Eight persons heeded God's warnings and so escaped the _____.

# Answers to Bible Quiz 9: The F List

1. In the book of Genesis, what did Joseph predict would impoverish his world?

   **Famine**

2. In the book of Acts, what did Agabus predict would hit the Roman world hard?

   **Famine**

3. Who preferred to send for Paul at his own convenience?   **Felix**

4. "They devoted themselves to the apostles' teaching and to the _____."

   **Fellowship**

5. In Mark 1:16-20, what did Jesus promise his disciples they would become?

   **Fishers of men**

6. How many years did David reign as king?   **40**

7. What word appears in older English Bibles refers to premarital sex?

   *Fornication*

8. In a parable in Luke, the rich _____ was told he would forfeit his very life that night.

   **Fool**

9. In Galatians 5, we read about nine characteristics of the _____ of the Spirit.

   **Fruit**

10. Eight persons heeded God's warnings and so escaped the_____.

    **Flood**

# Bible Quiz 10: The G List

1. We sing, "_____, _____, hallelujah!"

2. The name of only one New Testament book begins with *G*. True or false?

3. The name of only one Old Testament book begins with *G*. True or false?

4. "Unless a _____ of wheat falls to the earth and dies…"

5. Which wise Jewish teacher counseled leniency in dealing with the Christian threat?

6. Which territory lay north of Samaria?

7. Which language was most commonly spoken in the Roman Empire?

8. What was Sodom's companion city?

9. Where did Jesus and his disciples often meet for prayer?

10. Which word appears nearly 4400 times in the Bible?

## Answers to Bible Quiz 10: The G List

1. We sing, "_____, _____, hallelujah!"

    **Glory**

2. The name of only one New Testament book begins with *G*.

    **True—Galatians**

3. The name of only one Old Testament book begins with *G*.

    **True—Genesis**

4. "Unless a _____ of wheat falls to the earth and dies…"

    **Grain**

5. Which wise Jewish teacher counseled leniency in dealing with the Christian threat?

    **Gamaliel**

6. Which territory lay north of Samaria?

    **Galilee**

7. Which language was most commonly spoken in the Roman Empire?

    **Greek**

8. What was Sodom's companion city?

    **Gomorrah**

9. Where did Jesus and his disciples often meet for prayer?

    **Gethsemane**

10. Which word appears nearly 4400 times in the Bible?

    **God**

# Bible Quiz 11: The H List

1. This city was Abraham's home for a while.

2. Which three minor prophets' names begin with *H*?

3. Judas went out and _____ himself.

4. What was Esther's other name?

5. "Do not _____ your brother in your heart" (Leviticus 19:17).

6. What name for the realm of the dead begins with *H*?

7. Noah's three sons were Shem, Japheth, and _____.

8. "Put on the _____ of salvation" (Ephesians 6:17).

9. What musical instrument is mentioned more than 25 times in the Bible?

10. Who ordered the execution of infant boys in the region of Bethlehem no later than 4 BC?

# Answers to Bible Quiz 11: The H List

1. This city was Abraham's home for a while.

   **Haran**

2. Which three minor prophets' names begin with *H*?

   **Hosea, Habakkuk, and Haggai**

3. Judas went out and _____ himself.

   **Hanged**

4. What was Esther's other name?

   **Hadassah**

5. "Do not _____ your brother in your heart" (Leviticus 19:17).

   **Hate**

6. What name for the realm of the dead begins with *H*?

   **Hades**

7. Noah's three sons were Shem, Japheth, and _____.

   **Ham**

8. "Put on the _____ of salvation" (Ephesians 6:17).

   **Helmet**

9. What musical instrument is mentioned more than 25 times in the Bible?

   **The harp**

10. Who ordered the execution of infant boys in the region of Bethlehem no later than 4 BC?

    **Herod the Great**

# Bible Quiz 12: The I List

1. The largest city of the Roman Empire, with a population of more than one million, was in which nation?

2. Which sin is forbidden in the final verse of 1 John?

3. What Hebrew word means "God with us"?

4. "The perishable must clothe itself with the _____" (1 Corinthians 15:53).

5. The firstborn received a double share of the _____.

6. To extricate himself from a tight situation, David feigned _____ in the presence of the Philistine king.

7. _____ with foreigners (noncovenant people) was strictly forbidden in the Old Testament.

8. Who was Abraham's second son?

9. Who was Abraham's first son (but not his heir)?

10. Solomon's throne was made of gold and _____.

## Answers to Bible Quiz 12: The I List

1. The largest city of the Roman Empire, with a population of more than one million, was in which nation?

   **Italy**

2. Which sin is forbidden in the final verse of 1 John?

   **Idolatry**

3. What Hebrew word means "God with us"?

   *Immanuel*

4. "The perishable must clothe itself with the _____" (1 Corinthians 15:53).

   **Imperishable**

5. The firstborn received a double share of the _____.

   **Inheritance**

6. To extricate himself from a tight situation, David feigned _____ in the presence of the Philistine king.

   **Insanity**

7. _____ with foreigners (noncovenant people) was strictly forbidden in the Old Testament.

   **Intermarriage**

8. Who was Abraham's second son?

   **Isaac**

9. Who was Abraham's first son (but not his heir)?

   **Ishmael**

10. Solomon's throne was made of gold and _____.

    **Ivory**

# Bible Quiz 13: The J List

1. How many of Jesus' 12 apostles had names starting with the letter *J*?

2. What Hebrew letter is usually transcribed as *j* in English: *iota*, *yodh*, or *jabba*?

3. "Will not the _____ of all the earth do right?" Abraham asked in Genesis 18:25.

4. Who sacrificed his daughter as a burnt offering?

5. Who endured much suffering because of Satan and because of his three so-called friends?

6. What city was also called Salem?

7. The long-lost Book of the Law was discovered during whose reign?

8. Samson struck down 1000 Philistines with a donkey's _____.

9. Which Bible book has 52 chapters? (Hint: The author also wrote Lamentations.)

10. The house of Simon the Tanner was located in the coastal city of _____ (Acts 10).

# Answers to Bible Quiz 13: The J List

1. How many of Jesus' 12 apostles had names starting with the letter *J*?

   **Five: James and John (the sons of Zebedee), James (the son of Alphaeus), Judas Iscariot, and Judas son of James (also called Thaddaeus).**

2. What Hebrew letter is usually transcribed as *j* in English?

   **Yodh. Iota is Greek, and Jabba is a Hutt.**

3. "Will not the _____ of all the earth do right?" Abraham asked in Genesis 18:25.

   **Judge**

4. Who sacrificed his daughter as a burnt offering?

   **Jephthah**

5. Who endured much suffering because of Satan and because of his three so-called friends?

   **Job**

6. What city was also called Salem?

   **Jerusalem**

7. The long-lost Book of the Law was discovered during whose reign?

   **Josiah**

8. Samson struck down 1000 Philistines with a donkey's _____.

   **Jawbone**

9. Which Bible book has 52 chapters?

   **Jeremiah**

10. The house of Simon the Tanner was located in the coastal city of _____ (Acts 10).

    **Joppa**

# Bible Quiz 14: The K List

1. Peter was to be given the _____ of the kingdom of heaven.

2. Who was the father of King Saul?

3. "Am I my brother's _____?" complained Cain.

4. What valley separates Jerusalem from the Mount of Olives?

5. Judas betrayed the Son of Man with a _____.

6. Who led a rebellion against Moses in Numbers 16?

7. "_____ and the door will be opened to you."

8. Levi had three sons: Gershom, Merari, and _____.

9. The meat of the Passover meal was from a lamb or a _____.

10. What bird was listed in Leviticus as one of the unclean foods?

# Answers to Bible Quiz 14: The K List

1. Peter was to be given the _____ of the kingdom of heaven.

   **Keys**

2. Who was the father of King Saul?

   **Kish**

3. "Am I my brother's _____?" complained Cain.

   **Keeper**

4. What valley separates Jerusalem from the Mount of Olives?

   **Kidron**

5. Judas betrayed the Son of Man with a _____.

   **Kiss**

6. Who led a rebellion against Moses in Numbers 16?

   **Korah**

7. "_____ and the door will be opened to you."

   **Knock**

8. Levi had three sons: Gershom, Merari, and _____.

   **Kohath**

9. The meat of the Passover meal was from a lamb or a _____.

   **Kid (a young goat)**

10. What bird was listed in Leviticus as one of the unclean foods?

    **The kite (Leviticus 11:14)**

# Bible Quiz 15: The L List

1. Who was the father of Ammon and Moab?

2. Whose wife looked back and became a pillar of salt?

3. Who employed Jacob for more than 20 years?

4. Who was Jacob's first wife?

5. What book comes just before Ezekiel?

6. Who was rebuked for their materialism in Revelation 3?

7. Jehu turned the temple of Baal into a _____.

8. What do *lamed* and *lambda* have in common?

9. "Faint with love" appears only in Song of Solomon and is rendered "_____" in the NASB.

10. "_____, come out!"

# Answers to Bible Quiz 15: The L List

1. Who was the father of Ammon and Moab?

    **Lot**

2. Whose wife looked back and became a pillar of salt?

    **Lot**

3. Who employed Jacob for more than 20 years?

    **Laban**

4. Who was Jacob's first wife?

    **Leah**

5. What book comes just before Ezekiel?

    **Lamentations**

6. Who was rebuked for their materialism in Revelation 3?

    **Laodicea**

7. Jehu turned the temple of Baal into a _____.

    **Latrine**

8. What do *lamed* and *lambda* have in common?

    **They are the names of the letter *l* in Hebrew and Greek, respectively.**

9. "Faint with love" appears only in Song of Solomon and is rendered "_____" in the NASB.

    **lovesick**

10. "_____, come out!"

    **Lazarus**

# Bible Quiz 16: The M List

1. Who was the oldest person recorded in the Bible?

2. Ezekiel saw a vision concerning Gog and _____.

3. What does the name *Adam* mean?

4. How many New Testament books have names that begin with the letter *M*?

5. How many Old Testament books have names that begin with the letter *M*?

6. The sons of Lot were Ammon and _____.

7. Name the high priest's servant whose ear Peter lopped off.

8. Who is the archangel?

9. What body of water was called "the Great Sea" in the Old Testament?

10. Who was the sister of Moses and Aaron?

# Answers to Bible Quiz 16: The M List

1. Who was the oldest person recorded in the Bible?

    **Methuselah**

2. Ezekiel saw a vision concerning Gog and _____.

    **Magog**

3. What does the name *Adam* mean?

    **Man or mankind**

4. How many New Testament books have names that begin with the letter *M*?

    **Two—Matthew and Mark**

5. How many Old Testament books have names that begin with the letter *M*?

    **Two—Micah and Malachi**

6. The sons of Lot were Ammon and _____.

    **Moab**

7. Name the high priest's servant whose ear Peter lopped off.

    **Malchus**

8. Who is the archangel?

    **Michael. His name means "Who is like God?" (*Mi* = who, *ke* = like, *el* = God)**

9. What body of water was called "the Great Sea" in the Old Testament?

    **The Mediterranean**

10. Who was the sister of Moses and Aaron?

    **Miriam**

# Bible Quiz 17: The N List

1. Who was the leprous commander of the army of Syria (or Aram)?

2. What was Jesus' hometown?

3. Who munched grass in Daniel 4?

4. Whom did Jesus see under the sycamore-fig tree?

5. Who came to Jesus at night?

6. Who was Joshua's father?

7. "We brought_____ into the world, and we can take _____ out of it" (1 Timothy 6:7).

8. Tough question: Who was the false prophetess mentioned in the book of Nehemiah?

9. Tough question: What was the name of the priestly village on the Mount of Olives, opposite Jerusalem?

10. Who was Ruth's mother-in-law?

# Answers to Bible Quiz 17: The N List

1. Who was the leprous commander of the army of Syria (or Aram)?

    **Naaman**

2. What was Jesus' hometown?

    **Nazareth**

3. Who munched grass in Daniel 4?

    **Nebuchadnezzar**

4. Whom did Jesus see under the sycamore-fig tree?

    **Nathanael**

5. Who came to Jesus at night?

    **Nicodemus**

6. Who was Joshua's father?

    **Nun**

7. "We brought_____ into the world, and we can take _____ out of it" (1 Timothy 6:7).

    **Nothing**

8. Tough question: Who was the false prophetess mentioned in the book of Nehemiah?

    **Noadiah**

9. Tough question: What was the name of the priestly village on the Mount of Olives, opposite Jerusalem?

    **Nob**

10. Who was Ruth's mother-in-law?

    **Naomi**

# Bible Quiz 18: The O List

1. This is a common tree in the Middle East.

2. Who was one of the Judges (and Caleb's nephew)?

3. Who was Philemon's runaway slave?

4. Who is the only minor prophet whose name begins with *O*?

5. What is the last letter of the Greek alphabet?

6. What is the fifteenth letter of the Greek alphabet? (Hint: It's closely related to the last letter.)

7. Absalom got his head caught in the branches of this tree.

8. "They _____ him by the blood of the Lamb and by the word of their testimony" (Revelation 12:11).

9. Prophets, priests, and kings were anointed with _____.

10. "_____ wide your hearts," Paul pled in 2 Corinthians 6:13.

# Answers to Bible Quiz 18: The O List

1. This is a common tree in the Middle East.

   Olive

2. Who was one of the Judges (and Caleb's nephew)?

   Othniel

3. Who was Philemon's runaway slave?

   Onesimus

4. Who is the only minor prophet whose name begins with *O*?

   Obadiah

5. What is the last letter of the Greek alphabet?

   Omega—big *O*

6. What is the fifteenth letter of the Greek alphabet? (Hint: It's closely related to the last letter.)

   Omicron—little *o*

7. Absalom got his head caught in the branches of this tree.

   Oak

8. "They _____ him by the blood of the Lamb and by the word of their testimony" (Revelation 12:11).

   Overcame

9. Prophets, priests, and kings were anointed with _____.

   Oil

10. "_____ wide your hearts," Paul pled in 2 Corinthians 6:13.

    Open

# Bible Quiz 19: The P List

1. This word means "a comparison" and is a name for an earthly story containing a heavenly meaning.

2. What festival is celebrated on the fourteenth of Nisan?

3. What English word, featured in the title of a 2004 movie, literally means "suffering"?

4. What was the island of John's exile?

5. Whose old name was Saul?

6. "When you are _____ in one place, flee to another" (Matthew 10:23).

7. Name two of the seven churches addressed in Revelation.

8. _____ Festus succeeded Felix.

9. The name of this festival comes from the Greek word for 50.

10. "No one who puts his hand to the _____ and looks back is fit for service" (Luke 9:62).

# Answers to Bible Quiz 19: The P List

1. This word means "a comparison" and is a name for an earthly story containing a heavenly meaning.

   *Parable*

2. What festival is celebrated on the fourteenth of Nisan?

   **Passover**

3. What English word, featured in the title of a 2004 movie, literally means "suffering"?

   *Passion*

4. What was the island of John's exile?

   **Patmos**

5. Whose old name was Saul?

   **Paul**

6. "When you are _____ in one place, flee to another" (Matthew 10:23).

   **Persecuted**

7. Name two of the seven churches addressed in Revelation.

   **Pergamum and Philadelphia**

8. _____ Festus succeeded Felix.

   **Porcius**

9. The name of this festival comes from the Greek word for 50.

   **Pentecost**

10. "No one who puts his hand to the _____ and looks back is fit for service" (Luke 9:62).

    **Plow**

# Bible Quiz 20: The Q List

1. How many books of the Bible have names that begin with *Q*?

2. In Exodus 5, the Egyptian slave drivers toughened the work without reducing the _____.

3. When the Israelites craved meat, the Lord sent them this bird—until it came out of their nostrils! (See Numbers 11:20.)

4. The _____ of Sheba visited Solomon and asked him many difficult questions.

5. Who was the governor of Syria when Jesus was born: Quartus, Quirinius, Queequeg, or Quadrans?

6. What is the name of the monastic community where the Dead Sea Scrolls were discovered in the 1940s and '50s?

7. According to the evidence of archaeological discoveries, what was the name of the national god of the nation of Edom: Qarqar, Qindar, Qos, or Qaid?

8. Psalm 127 speaks of the advantages of having many sons. Solomon wrote, "Blessed is the man whose _____ is full of them" (verse 5).

9. Jude speaks of the godless persons who "are blemishes at your love feasts, eating with you without the slightest _____, shepherds who feed only themselves" (verse 12).

10. "Esau became a skillful hunter...while Jacob was a _____ man, staying among the tents" (Genesis 25:27).

# Answers to Bible Quiz 20: The Q List

1. How many books of the Bible have names that begin with *Q*?

   **None**

2. In Exodus 5, the Egyptian slave drivers toughened the work without reducing the _____.   **Quota**

3. When the Israelites craved meat, the Lord sent them this bird—until it came out of their nostrils! (See Numbers 11:20.)   **Quail**

4. The _____ of Sheba visited Solomon and asked him many difficult questions.

   **Queen**

5. Who was the governor of Syria when Jesus was born?   **Quirinius**

6. What is the name of the monastic community where the Dead Sea Scrolls were discovered in the 1940s and '50s?

   **Qumran**

7. According to the evidence of archaeological discoveries, what was the name of the national god of the nation of Edom?   **Qos**

8. Psalm 127 speaks of the advantages of having many sons. Solomon wrote, "Blessed is the man whose_____ is full of them" (verse 5).

   **Quiver**

9. Jude speaks of the godless persons who "are blemishes at your love feasts, eating with you without the slightest _____, shepherds who feed only themselves" (verse 12).

   **Qualm**

10. "Esau became a skillful hunter...while Jacob was a _____ man, staying among the tents" (Genesis 25:27).

   **Quiet**

# Bible Quiz 21: The R List

1. Who hid the spies in Jericho?

2. Who was Moses' father-in-law?

3. What Aramaic term of contempt did Jesus refer to in Matthew 5?

4. "But you are not to be called _____" (Matthew 23:8). (Hint: This is a title that occurs 15 times in the New Testament.)

5. Numbers 16 records Korah's _____ against Moses.

6. What animal did the Philistines evidently consider sacred (1 Samuel 6:4)?

7. What is the Hebrew word for "wind, breath, or spirit": *rubba*, *ruah*, *raqu*, or *rupu*?

8. What is another name for the coney or hyrax (Leviticus 11:5)?

9. All the following words appear in the Bible except which one?

    robe

    robber

    ruler

    ring

    ram

    rape

    rhythm

    revelation

    route

10. What requirement for salvation begins with *r*?

# Answers to Bible Quiz 21: The R List

1. Who hid the spies in Jericho?

   **Rahab**

2. Who was Moses' father-in-law?

   **Reuel**

3. What Aramaic term of contempt did Jesus refer to in Matthew 5?

   ***Raca***

4. "But you are not to be called _____" (Matthew 23:8).

   **Rabbi**

5. Numbers 16 records Korah's _____ against Moses.

   **Rebellion**

6. What animal did the Philistines evidently consider sacred (1 Samuel 6:4)?

   **Rat**

7. What is the Hebrew word for "wind, breath, or spirit"?

   ***Ruah***

8. What is another name for the coney or hyrax (Leviticus 11:5)?

   **Rock badger**

9. All the following words appear in the Bible except which one?

   **Rhythm**

10. What requirement for salvation begins with *r*?

   **Repentance**

# Bible Quiz 22: The S List

1. The seventh day of the Jewish week is the _____.

2. Onesimus had been Philemon's_____.

3. "_____the rod and _____ the child" is a common paraphrase of Proverbs 22:15 and similar verses.

4. What did people of Ephraim say if they couldn't pronounce the word *shibboleth* (Judges 12:6)?

5. One of the 12 tribes of Israel has a name that begins with *S*. What is it?

6. What is the twenty-second book of the Bible?

7. What is the ethnicity of the bride in the twenty-second book of the Bible?

8. Where did Paul plan to go after visiting Rome (Romans 15)?

9. What is the "greater light" of Genesis 1?

10. Who was Nehemiah's enemy?

# Answers to Bible Quiz 22: The S List

1. The seventh day of the Jewish week is the _____.

   **Sabbath**

2. Onesimus had been Philemon's _____.

   **Slave**

3. "_____ the rod and _____ the child" is a common paraphrase of Proverbs 22:15 and similar verses.

   **Spare...spoil**

4. What did people of Ephraim say if they couldn't pronounce the word *shibboleth* (Judges 12:6)?

   ***Sibboleth***

5. One of the 12 tribes of Israel has a name that begins with *S*. What is it?

   **Simeon**

6. What is the twenty-second book of the Bible?

   **Song of Songs**

7. What is the ethnicity of the bride in the twenty-second book of the Bible?

   **Shulammite. See Song of Songs 6:15.**

8. Where did Paul plan to go after visiting Rome (Romans 15)?

   **Spain**

9. What is the "greater light" of Genesis 1?

   **The sun**

10. Who was Nehemiah's enemy?

    **Sanballat**

# Bible Quiz 23: The T List

1. Old Testament priests used the Urim and the _____ to ascertain God's will.

2. Tigers are found in the Bible. True or false?

3. During the Feast of _____, the Israelites celebrated their journey out of Egypt.

4. Paul wrote one letter to a young pastor named _____.

5. What is the New Testament Greek word for *three*: *tria*, *ter*, *tres*, or *thrix*?

6. Which musical instrument is found in the Bible: tuba, trumpet, trombone, or timpani?

7. "Come...see...go..._____" (Matthew 28:6-7).

8. "Do not put the Lord your God to the _____" (Matthew 4:7).

9. Paul pled with the Lord to remove his _____ in the flesh (2 Corinthians 12:7-8).

10. "Nor are you to be called _____" (Matthew 23:10).

# Answers to Bible Quiz 23: The T List

1. Old Testament priests used the Urim and the _____ to ascertain God's will.

   **Thummim**

2. Tigers are found in the Bible.

   **False**

3. During the Feast of _____, the Israelites celebrated their journey out of Egypt.

   **Tabernacles**

4. Paul wrote one letter to a young pastor named _____.

   **Titus**

5. What is the New Testament Greek word for *three*: *tria*, *ter*, *tres*, or *thrix*?

   **Tria**

6. Which musical instrument is found in the Bible: tuba, trumpet, trombone, or timpani?

   **Trumpet**

7. "Come…see…go…_____" (Matthew 28:6-7).

   **Tell**

8. "Do not put the Lord your God to the _____" (Matthew 4:7).

   **Test**

9. Paul pled with the Lord to remove his _____ in the flesh (2 Corinthians 12:7-8).

   **Thorn**

10. "Nor are you to be called _____" (Matthew 23:10).

    **Teacher**

# Bible Quiz 24: The U List

1. Old Testament priests used the _____ and the Thummim to ascertain God's will.

2. Some Jews were astonished because Peter and John were courageous and were "_____, ordinary men" (Acts 4:13).

3. Zechariah's staffs were called Favor and _____ (Zechariah 11:7).

4. Bathsheba's husband was _____ the Hittite.

5. The wailing at funerals in the Middle East in biblical times (and today) is called _____.

6. The Last Supper took place in an _____ room.

7. Who died for irreverently trying to stabilize the ark of the covenant?

8. What city is the original home of Abram's family?

9. The southern part of Egypt was called "_____ Egypt."

10. Charging of interest, or _____, was forbidden under Old Testament law.

# Answers to Bible Quiz 24: The U List

1. Old Testament priests used the _____ and the Thummim to ascertain God's will.

   **Urim**

2. Some Jews were astonished because Peter and John were courageous and were "_____, ordinary men" (Acts 4:13).

   **Unschooled**

3. Zechariah's staffs were called Favor and _____ (Zechariah 11:7).

   **Union**

4. Bathsheba's husband was _____ the Hittite.

   **Uriah**

5. The wailing at funerals in the Middle East in biblical times (and today) is called _____.

   **Ululation**

6. The Last Supper took place in an _____ room.

   **Upper**

7. Who died for irreverently trying to stabilize the ark of the covenant?

   **Uzzah**

8. What city is the original home of Abram's family?

   **Ur**

9. The southern part of Egypt was called "_____ Egypt."

   **Upper**

10. Charging of interest, or _____, was forbidden under Old Testament law.

    **Usury**

# Bible Quiz 25: The V List

1. "Though I walk through the _____ of the shadow of death…" (Psalm 23:4).

2. Who preceded Esther as the queen of Persian King Ahasuerus (Xerxes)?

3. What is the other name for the Hebrew letter *waw*?

4. Jesus' mother is referred to as the _____ Mary.

5. Catholic theology distinguishes between _____ and mortal sins.

6. What bird is mentioned ten times in the Bible?

7. Women generally wore _____ in public in Bible times.

8. "When you make a _____ to God, do not delay in fulfilling it" (Ecclesiastes 5:4).

9. The Bible has more than 30,000 of these.

10. If one obeyed Song of Songs 2:15 (catching the little foxes) and killed his quarry, what would he be guilty of: vulpicide, varricide, vaxicide, or velocide?

# Answers to Bible Quiz 25: The V List

1. "Though I walk through the _____ of the shadow of death…" (Psalm 23:4).

   **Valley**

2. Who preceded Esther as the queen of Persian King Ahasuerus (Xerxes)?

   **Vashti**

3. What is the other name for the Hebrew letter *waw*?

   ***Vav***

4. Jesus' mother is referred to as the _____ Mary.

   **Virgin**

5. Catholic theology distinguishes between _____ and mortal sins.

   **Venial**

6. What bird is mentioned ten times in the Bible?

   **Vulture**

7. Women generally wore _____ in public in Bible times.

   **Veils**

8. "When you make a _____ to God, do not delay in fulfilling it" (Ecclesiastes 5:4).

   **Vow**

9. The Bible has more than 30,000 of these.

   **Verses**

10. If one obeyed Song of Songs 2:15 (catching the little foxes) and killed his quarry, what would he be guilty of: vulpicide, varricide, vaxicide, or velocide?

    **Vulpicide**

# Bible Quiz 26: The W List

1. In the Middle East, an intermittent stream is usually called a _____.

2. The Communion elements include bread and _____.

3. "The _____ of sin is death" (Romans 6:23).

4. What is the other name for the Hebrew letter *vav*?

5. Jesus made a _____ out of cords.

6. What was Rahab and Gomer's vocation?

7. Who visited a little boy in Bethlehem?

8. Who uses a sheepskin as a disguise?

9. "Where their _____ never dies..."

10. What did Jacob and the angel of the Lord do until daybreak?

# Answers to Bible Quiz 26: The W List

1. In the Middle East, an intermittent stream is usually called a
   _____.

   **Wadi**

2. The Communion elements include bread and _____.

   **Wine**

3. "The _____ of sin is death" (Romans 6:23).

   **Wages**

4. What is the other name for the Hebrew letter *vav*?

   **Waw**

5. Jesus made a _____ out of cords.

   **Whip**

6. What was Rahab and Gomer's vocation?

   **Whoredom**

7. Who visited a little boy in Bethlehem?

   **The wise men**

8. Who uses a sheepskin as a disguise?

   **A wolf**

9. "Where their _____ never dies..."

   **Worm**

10. What did Jacob and the angel of the Lord do until daybreak?

    **Wrestle**

# Bible Quiz 27: The X List

*(All answers include the letter x but may not begin with x.)*

1. What Persian king is mentioned 30 times in Esther and once in Daniel?

2. "You shall not covet...your neighbor's _____ (Exodus 20:17).

3. "_____ your thoughts on Jesus" (Hebrews 3:1). "Let us _____ our eyes on Jesus" (Hebrews 12:2).

4. "After three months, we put out to sea in a ship that had wintered in the island. It was an Alexandrian ship with the figurehead of the twin gods Castor and _____" (Acts 28:11).

5. "_____ was afraid and said, 'That's enough for now'" (Acts 24:25).

6. "But the _____ collector stood at a distance" (Luke 18:13).

7. "[Jesus] replied, 'Go tell that _____, I will drive out demons and heal people today and tomorrow'" (Luke 13:32).

8. "The _____ is already at the root of the trees" (Luke 3:9).

9. "A curse on him who is _____ in doing the LORD's work" (Jeremiah 48:10).

10. In the New Testament Greek alphabet, *x* is called _____.

# Answers to Bible Quiz 27: The X List

1. What Persian king is mentioned 30 times in Esther and once in Daniel?

    **Xerxes**

2. "You shall not covet…your neighbor's _____ (Exodus 20:17).

    **Ox**

3. "_____ your thoughts on Jesus" (Hebrews 3:1). "Let us _____ our eyes on Jesus" (Hebrews 12:2).

    **Fix**

4. "After three months, we put out to sea in a ship that had wintered in the island. It was an Alexandrian ship with the figurehead of the twin gods Castor and _____" (Acts 28:11).

    **Pollux**

5. "_____ was afraid and said, 'That's enough for now'" (Acts 24:25).

    **Felix**

6. "But the _____ collector stood at a distance" (Luke 18:13).

    **Tax**

7. "[Jesus] replied, 'Go tell that _____, I will drive out demons and heal people today and tomorrow'" (Luke 13:32).

    **Fox**

8. "The _____ is already at the root of the trees" (Luke 3:9).    **Ax**

9. "A curse on him who is _____ in doing the LORD's work" (Jeremiah 48:10).

    **Lax**

10. In the New Testament Greek alphabet, *x* is called _____.    *Xi*

# Bible Quiz 28: The Y List

1. "Jesus Christ is the same _____ and today and forever" (Hebrews 13:8).

2. "Don't let anyone look down on you because you are _____ (1 Timothy 4:12).

3. What common pronoun appears some 13,000 times in the English Bible?

4. Which one of these words appears in the Bible: *yam*, *yak*, *yeast*, or *yahoo*?

5. Which of the following begins with a *Y* sound in Hebrew: *Moses*, *Judah*, *Haman*, or *Arabah*?

6. How many books of the Bible have names that begin with the letter *Y*?

7. What is God's covenant name in the Old Testament?

8. "In the four hundred and eightieth _____ after the Israelites had come out of Egypt…" (1 Kings 6:1).

9. How else can the personal name *Syzygus* be translated (Philippians 4:3)?

10. "For no matter how many promises God has made, they are _____ in Christ" (2 Corinthians 1:20).

# Answers to Bible Quiz 28: The Y List

1. "Jesus Christ is the same _____ and today and forever"
   (Hebrews 13:8).

   **Yesterday**

2. "Don't let anyone look down on you because you are _____ "
   (1 Timothy 4:12).

   **Young**

3. What common pronoun appears some 13,000 times in the English
   Bible?

   **You**

4. Which one of these words appears in the Bible: *yam, yak, yeast,* or
   *yahoo*?   **Yeast**

5. Which of the following begins with a *Y* sound in Hebrew: *Moses,*
   *Judah, Haman,* or *Arabah*?

   **Judah**

6. How many books of the Bible have names that begin with the
   letter *Y*?   **None**

7. What is God's covenant name in the Old Testament?   **Yahweh**

8. "In the four hundred and eightieth _____ after the Israelites had
   come out of Egypt..." (1 Kings 6:1).

   **Year**

9. How else can the personal name *Syzygus* be translated (Philippians
   4:3)?

   **Yokefellow**

10. "For no matter how many promises God has made, they are
    _____ in Christ" (2 Corinthians 1:20).   **Yes**

# Bible Quiz 29: The Z List

1. Who was governor of Judah in Haggai 1:14?

2. What is one of the deserts in which the Israelites spent their 40 years wandering?

3. What is another name for Jerusalem?

4. Several years after the birth of Christ, what was the year that never was?

5. Who was king of northern Israel for a whopping seven days (1 Kings 16:15)?

6. What is another name for the Rephaites (Deuteronomy 2:20)?

7. In Numbers 26, 27, and 36, this man had only daughters, so they each received an inheritance in the Promised Land.

8. What two minor prophets have names that begin with *Z*?

9. What Philistine city was given to David when he was on the run from Saul?

10. Who was the father of James and John?

# Answers to Bible Quiz 29: The Z List

1. Who was governor of Judah in Haggai 1:14?

   **Zerubbabel**

2. What is one of the deserts in which the Israelites spent their 40 years wandering?

   **Zin**

3. What is another name for Jerusalem?

   **Zion**

4. Several years after the birth of Christ, what was the year that never was?

   **Zero**

5. Who was king of northern Israel for a whopping seven days (1 Kings 16:15)?

   **Zimri**

6. What is another name for the Rephaites (Deuteronomy 2:20)?

   **Zamzummim or Zamzummites**

7. In Numbers 26, 27, and 36, this man had only daughters, so they each received an inheritance in the Promised Land.

   **Zelophehad**

8. What two minor prophets have names that begin with *Z*?

   **Zephaniah and Zechariah**

9. What Philistine city was given to David when he was on the run from Saul?

   **Ziklag**

10. Who was the father of James and John?

    **Zebedee**

# Books of the Bible

### Bible Quiz 30: Genesis

1. Whose name also means "mankind"?

2. Who were Cain's two brothers?

3. Where was the enormous tower built against the Lord's will?

4. How many chapters does Genesis have: 30, 40, 50, or 60?

5. What language was Genesis written in?

6. What other language—used in 1 percent of the Old Testament—is found in a single verse of Genesis?

7. How many feet long was Noah's Ark: 150, 450, 1050, or 1750?

8. Which of the following characters does not appear in Genesis: Abraham, Goliath, Ishmael, or Joseph?

9. How many sons did Jacob have?

10. Which New Testament book starts with the same three words that Genesis begins with?

# Answers to Bible Quiz 30: Genesis

1. Whose name also means "mankind"?

   **Adam**

2. Who were Cain's two brothers?

   **Abel and Seth**

3. Where was the enormous tower built against the Lord's will?

   **Babel**

4. How many chapters does Genesis have: 30, 40, 50, or 60?

   **50**

5. What language was Genesis written in?

   **Hebrew**

6. What other language—used in 1 percent of the Old Testament—is found in a single verse of Genesis?

   **Aramaic**

7. How many feet long was Noah's Ark: 150, 450, 1050, or 1750?

   **450**

8. Which of the following characters does not appear in Genesis: Abraham, Goliath, Ishmael, or Joseph?

   **Goliath**

9. How many sons did Jacob have?

   **12**

10. Which New Testament book starts with the same three words that Genesis begins with?

    **John**

# Bible Quiz 31: Exodus

1. Who is the central figure of Exodus?

2. How many chapters are in Exodus: 20, 40, 60, or 80?

3. Who led Egypt?

4. Finally, at the end of Exodus, the _____ has been constructed.

5. Who was Zipporah?

6. What was Jethro's advice to Moses in Exodus 18?

7. In which chapter do we find the apostasy in connection with the golden calves: 2, 12, 22, or 32?

8. Who were Shiphrah and Puah?

9. In which chapter of Exodus do we find the Ten Commandments?

10. Which book follows Exodus?

# Answers to Bible Quiz 31: Exodus

1. Who is the central figure of Exodus?

   **Moses**

2. How many chapters are in Exodus: 20, 40, 60, or 80?

   **40**

3. Who led Egypt?

   **Pharaoh**

4. Finally, at the end of Exodus, the _____ has been constructed.

   **Tabernacle**

5. Who was Zipporah?

   **Moses' wife**

6. What was Jethro's advice to Moses in Exodus 18?

   **Delegate!**

7. In which chapter do we find the apostasy in connection with the golden calves: 2, 12, 22, or 32?

   **32**

8. Who were Shiphrah and Puah?

   **Hebrew midwives**

9. In which chapter of Exodus do we find the Ten Commandments?

   **20**

10. Which book follows Exodus?

    **Leviticus**

# Bible Quiz 32: Leviticus

1. The name *Leviticus* comes from *Levi*, the name of the priestly tribe that superintended the tabernacle and the sacrifices. True or false?

2. Leviticus has 27 chapters and precedes Deuteronomy. True or false?

3. Nadab and Abihu are struck dead in what chapter of Leviticus: 1, 10, 20, or 30?

4. Leviticus teaches that blood and fat are acceptable foods for Israelites. True or false?

5. The Levites diagnosed mildew and skin diseases. True or false?

6. "Love your neighbor as yourself" appears in Leviticus. True or false?

7. According to Leviticus 20:13, sodomy merits _____.

8. Israel will receive blessings or disasters depending on their obedience or disobedience according to what chapter in Leviticus: 6, 16, 26, or 66?

9. Leviticus 25 contains instructions concerning the Year of Jubilee. True or false?

10. Which one of these is the key word in Leviticus: *happy, holy, humane,* or *holistic?*

# Answers to Bible Quiz 32: Leviticus

1. The name *Leviticus* comes from *Levi*, the name of the priestly tribe that superintended the tabernacle and the sacrifices.   **True**

2. Leviticus has 27 chapters and precedes Deuteronomy.
    **True, though Numbers comes between them**

3. Nadab and Abihu are struck dead in what chapter of Leviticus: 1, 10, 20, or 30?   **10**

4. Leviticus teaches that blood and fat are acceptable foods for Israelites.
    **False**

5. The Levites diagnosed mildew and skin diseases.   **True**

6. "Love your neighbor as yourself" appears in Leviticus.   **True**

7. According to Leviticus 20:13, sodomy merits _____.   **Death**

8. Israel will receive blessings or disasters depending on their obedience or disobedience according to what chapter in Leviticus: 6, 16, 26, or 66?
    **26**

9. Leviticus 25 contains instructions concerning the Year of Jubilee.
    **True**

10. Which one of these is the key word in Leviticus: *happy, holy, humane,* or *holistic*?   **Holy**

# Bible Quiz 33: Numbers

1. The book of Numbers is set in what location: Egypt, the desert, Canaan, or Israel?

2. How many chapters are in Numbers: 16, 26, 36, or 46?

3. According to Numbers 12, what did God normally use to speak to the prophets: crystal balls, dreams, mystical sensations, or Urim and Thummim?

4. How many censuses are recorded in Numbers?

5. Which book precedes Numbers?

6. Who led a rebellion against Moses and Aaron: Koran, Konan, Kenan, or Kabzeel?

7. The Nazirite vow is found in Numbers. True or false?

8. The blessing of Aaron ("The LORD bless you and keep you") appears in which chapter of Numbers: 5, 6, 22, or 37?

9. What were the silver trumpets used for (Numbers 10): convening leaders' meetings, telling Israel to break camp, or musical entertainment?

10. When Moses strikes the rock in direct opposition to God's instructions, the much-desired water does not flow from it. True or false?

# Answers to Bible Quiz 33: Numbers

1. The book of Numbers is set in what location: Egypt, the desert, Canaan, or Israel?

   **The desert**

2. How many chapters are in Numbers: 16, 26, 36, or 46?  **36**

3. According to Numbers 12, what did God normally use to speak to the prophets: crystal balls, dreams, mystical sensations, or Urim and Thummim?

   **Dreams**

4. How many censuses are recorded in Numbers?  **Two**

5. Which book precedes Numbers?  **Leviticus**

6. Who led a rebellion against Moses and Aaron: Korah, Konan, Kenan, or Kabzeel?

   **Korah**

7. The Nazirite vow is found in Numbers.  **True**

8. The blessing of Aaron ("The LORD bless you and keep you") appears in which chapter of Numbers: 5, 6, 22, or 37?  **6**

9. What were the silver trumpets used for (Numbers 10): convening leaders' meetings, calling Israel to break camp, or musical entertainment?

   **Convening leaders' meetings and calling Israel to break camp**

10. When Moses strikes the rock in direct opposition to God's instructions, the much-desired water does not flow from it.

    **False**

# Bible Quiz 34: Deuteronomy

1. What is Deuteronomy's position in the Bible: fourth, fifth, sixth, or seventh?

2. In which chapter do we find the Decalogue?

3. The death of Moses is recorded in what chapter of Deuteronomy: 33, 34, 35, or 36?

4. Deuteronomy is the most quoted book of the Torah in the New Testament. True or false?

5. Deuteronomy 15:1 reads, "At the end of every seven years you must cancel _____."

6. Deuteronomy 18:15-19 (quoted in Acts 3:22-23) predicted that a prophet like Moses would come. That person was none other than _____.

7. "If a man guilty of a capital offense is put to death and his body is hung on a tree, you must not leave his body on the tree _____" (Deuteronomy 21:22-23).

8. Deuteronomy 23:15 says that a runaway slave must not be returned to his master. Did Paul feel obligated to follow this precept in the situation involving Onesimus and Philemon?

9. "Do not _____ an ox while it is treading out the grain" (Deuteronomy 24:5).

10. The book of Deuteronomy, which is largely a review of the wilderness wanderings, begins at the end of which year since the exodus?

# Answers to Bible Quiz 34: Deuteronomy

1. What is Deuteronomy's position in the Bible: fourth, fifth, sixth, or seventh? **Fifth**

2. In which chapter do we find the Decalogue? **5**

3. The death of Moses is recorded in what chapter of Deuteronomy: 33, 34, 35, or 36? **34**

4. Deuteronomy is the most quoted book of the Torah in the New Testament. **True**

5. Deuteronomy 15:1 reads, "At the end of every seven years you must cancel _____." **Debts**

6. Deuteronomy 18:15-19 (quoted in Acts 3:22-23) predicted that a prophet like Moses would come. That person was none other than _____. **Jesus Christ**

7. "If a man guilty of a capital offense is put to death and his body is hung on a tree, you must not leave his body on the tree _____" (Deuteronomy 21:22-23). **Overnight**

8. Deuteronomy 23:15 says that a runaway slave must not be returned to his master. Did Paul feel obligated to follow this precept in the situation involving Onesimus and Philemon? **No**

9. "Do not _____ an ox while it is treading out the grain" (Deuteronomy 24:5). **Muzzle**

10. The book of Deuteronomy, which is largely a review of the wilderness wanderings, begins at the end of which year since the exodus? **The fortieth and final year**

# Bible Quiz 35: Joshua

1. What was Joshua's other name?

2. Joshua was one of the 12 spies. True or false?

3. "Now Joshua son of Nun was filled with _____ because Moses had laid his hands on him. So the Israelites listened to him and did what the LORD had commanded Moses" (Deuteronomy 34:9).

4. What was the first city to fall in the conquest?

5. Which came first, the southern campaign or the northern campaign?

6. Who said, "As for me and my household, we will serve the LORD"?

7. What was Joshua's age at his death: 90, 110, 130, or 150?

8. The first attack against the city of Ai was successful. True or false?

9. Who pretended to be a distant people (rather than Canaanites) in order to avoid being attacked by Israel: the Jebusites, Gibeonites, Hittites, or Marmites?

10. Before Joshua died, the Lord repeatedly told him, "Be strong and _____."

## Answers to Bible Quiz 35: Joshua

1. What was Joshua's other name?
   **Hoshea (13:16)**

2. Joshua was one of the 12 spies.   **True**

3. "Now Joshua son of Nun was filled with _____ because Moses had laid his hands on him. So the Israelites listened to him and did what the LORD had commanded Moses" (Deuteronomy 34:9).
   **The spirit of wisdom**

4. What was the first city to fall in the conquest?   **Jericho**

5. Which came first, the southern campaign or the northern campaign?
   **Southern**

6. Who said, "As for me and my household, we will serve the LORD"?
   **Joshua**

7. What was Joshua's age at his death: 90, 110, 130, or 150?
   **110**

8. The first attack against the city of Ai was successful.
   **False**

9. Who pretended to be a distant people (rather than Canaanites) in order to avoid being attacked by Israel: the Jebusites, Gibeonites, Hittites, or Marmites?
   **Gibeonites**

10. Before Joshua died, the Lord repeatedly told him, "Be strong and _____."
    **Courageous**

# Bible Quiz 36: Judges

1. Which book comes before Judges?

2. Each judge led all the tribes of Israel when he or she judged. True or false?

3. Who was the strong man with a weakness for women?

4. Who defeated the Midianites even though he and his men were vastly outnumbered?

5. Who sacrificed his own daughter as a burnt offering in fulfillment of a vow?

6. Who was the first judge of Israel?

7. How many chapters are in the book of Judges?

8. Which judge assassinated the grossly obese Eglon, the Moabite oppressor of Israel?

9. Place the following significant women from the book of Judges in the order of their first mention: Delilah, Deborah, Jael, and Jephthah's daughter.

10. Which of the following is the final verse of Judges?

   • Then Samson prayed to the LORD, "O Sovereign LORD, remember me. O God, please strengthen me just once more, and let me with one blow get revenge on the Philistines for my two eyes."

   • "But grant me this one request," she said. "Give me two months to roam the hills and weep with my friends, because I will never marry."

   • In those days, Israel had no king; everyone did as he saw fit.

   • After the death of Joshua, the Israelites asked the LORD, "Who will be the first to go up and fight for us against the Canaanites?"

# Answers to Bible Quiz 36: Judges

1. Which book comes before Judges?

   **Joshua**

2. Each judge led all the tribes of Israel when he or she judged.

   **False**

3. Who was the strong man with a weakness for women?

   **Samson**

4. Who defeated the Midianites even though he and his men were vastly outnumbered?

   **Gideon**

5. Who sacrificed his own daughter as a burnt offering in fulfillment of a vow?

   **Jephthah**

6. Who was the first judge of Israel?

   **Othniel**

7. How many chapters are in the book of Judges?

   **21**

8. Which judge assassinated the grossly obese Eglon, the Moabite oppressor of Israel?

   **Ehud**

9. Place the following significant women from the book of Judges in the order of their first mention.

   **Deborah, Jael, Jephthah's daughter, Delilah**

10. Which of the following is the final verse of Judges?

    **"In those days, Israel had no king; everyone did as he saw fit" (Judges 21:25).**

# Bible Quiz 37: Ruth

1. The Dead Sea Scrolls include no manuscripts of Ruth. True or false?

2. Ruth's family fled to Moab from the famine that was ravaging Israel. True or false?

3. Which book of the Bible comes after Ruth?

4. In how many books of the Bible is Ruth mentioned (besides the book of Ruth)?

5. How many chapters does this short book contain?

6. Who was Ruth's mother-in-law?

7. About how many years did Ruth's mother-in-law live in Moab: 10, 20, 30, or 40?

8. To what city did Naomi return from Moab after the death of her husband?

9. Whom did the widow Ruth marry?

10. Who were Ruth's two most illustrious descendants?

# Answers to Bible Quiz 37: Ruth

1. The Dead Sea Scrolls include no manuscripts of Ruth.

   **False**

2. Ruth's family fled to Moab from the famine that was ravaging Israel.

   **False. Naomi's family fled. Ruth was already in Moab.**

3. Which book of the Bible comes after Ruth?

   **1 Samuel**

4. In how many books of the Bible is Ruth mentioned (besides the book of Ruth)?

   **One: Matthew**

5. How many chapters does this short book contain?

   **Four**

6. Who was Ruth's mother-in-law?

   **Naomi**

7. About how many years did Ruth's mother-in-law live in Moab: 10, 20, 30, or 40?

   **10**

8. To what city did Naomi return from Moab after the death of her husband?

   **Bethlehem**

9. Whom did the widow Ruth marry?

   **Boaz**

10. Who were Ruth's two most illustrious descendants?

    **David and Jesus Christ**

# Bible Quiz 38: 1 and 2 Samuel

1. In what capacity did Samuel serve Israel: prophet, king, priest, or military commander?

2. Which book comes after 2 Samuel?

3. Samuel was alive at the beginning of 1 Samuel and lived until the end of 2 Samuel. True or false?

4. Who was Israel's most common enemy in 1 and 2 Samuel?

5. How many chapters are in 1 and 2 Samuel combined: 40, 55, 65, or 80?

6. Which king of Israel died at the end of 1 Samuel?

7. Which character is not mentioned in 1 or 2 Samuel: Hannah, Goliath, Absalom, Caleb, or Solomon?

8. Who consulted a witch (a medium) in 1 Samuel 28?

9. Who was Joab?

10. Who feigned insanity in the presence of Achish, king of Gath?

## Answers to Bible Quiz 38: 1 and 2 Samuel

1. In what capacity did Samuel serve Israel: prophet, king, priest, or military commander?

   **Prophet and priest**

2. Which book comes after 2 Samuel?

   **1 Kings**

3. Samuel was alive at the beginning of 1 Samuel and lived until the end of 2 Samuel.

   **False. He was born in 1 Samuel 1, and he died in 1 Samuel 25. He is not alive in 2 Samuel at all.**

4. Who were Israel's most common enemies in 1 and 2 Samuel?

   **The Philistines**

5. How many chapters are in 1 and 2 Samuel combined: 40, 55, 65, or 80?

   **55**

6. Which king of Israel died at the end of 1 Samuel?

   **Saul**

7. Which character is not mentioned in 1 or 2 Samuel: Hannah, Goliath, Absalom, Caleb, or Solomon?

   **Caleb**

8. Who consulted a witch (a medium) in 1 Samuel 28?

   **Saul**

9. Who was Joab?

   **David's nephew and the commander of his army**

10. Who feigned insanity in the presence of Achish, king of Gath?

    **David**

# Bible Quiz 39: 1 and 2 Kings

1. After a foiled *coup d'etat*, who takes the throne at the beginning of 1 Kings?

2. What was the initial leadership style of Solomon's son and successor? What happened as a result?

3. The northern kingdom officially began around 931 BC. We read of this development in what chapter: 1 Kings 31, 1 Kings 12, 1 Kings 29, or 2 Kings 5?

4. How did Hiram help Solomon?

5. Elijah is mentioned in 1 Kings. True or false?

6. Elisha is mentioned in 1 Kings. True or false?

7. Who arranged the death of Naboth so that King Ahab could seize his property?

8. Which king and commander slaughtered the Baal worshippers?

9. How does 2 Kings end?

   The Assyrians overrun Israel (the northern kingdom).

   The Babylonians destroy Jerusalem and take Judah captive.

   Josiah's men find the long-lost Book of the Law.

   None of the above.

10. Who were the perennial enemies of Israel in these books?

# Answers to Bible Quiz 39: 1 and 2 Kings

1. After a foiled *coup d'etat*, who takes the throne at the beginning of 1 Kings?

    **Solomon**

2. What was the initial leadership style of Solomon's son and successor? What happened as a result?

    **He was harsh! The people were disheartened, and this led to Israel dividing into two nations.**

3. The northern kingdom officially began around 931 BC. We read of this development in what chapter: 1 Kings 31, 1 Kings 12, 1 Kings 29, or 2 Kings 5?

    **1 Kings 12**

4. How did Hiram help Solomon?

    **He provided materials for the construction of the temple.**

5. Elijah is mentioned in 1 Kings.

    **True**

6. Elisha is mentioned in 1 Kings.   **True**

7. Who arranged the death of Naboth so that King Ahab could seize his property?

    **Queen Jezebel**

8. Which king and commander slaughtered the Baal worshippers?

    **Jehu**

9. How does 2 Kings end?

    **The Babylonians destroy Jerusalem and take Judah captive.**

10. Who were the perennial enemies of Israel in these books?

    **The Arameans (Syrians)**

# Bible Quiz 40: 1 and 2 Chronicles

1. The books of 1 and 2 Kings focus on the history of the northern kingdom (Israel) and the southern kingdom (Judah). The books of 1 and 2 Chronicles focus primarily on what nation: Israel, Judah, Egypt, or Assyria?

2. What is the first word of 1 Chronicles: *David*, *Adam*, *Seth*, or *The*?

3. Who succeeds David as king at the end of 1 Chronicles?

4. How many chapters are in 1 and 2 Chronicles combined: 55, 65, 75, or 85?

5. Chronicles was the last book of the Hebrew Old Testament. True or false?

6. Who destroyed Jerusalem at the end of 2 Chronicles?

7. In the last three verses of 2 Chronicles, 70 years elapse and a decree is made. What is the decree?

8. In 2 Chronicles 26, King Uzziah becomes angry when challenged by 80 priests. What did they challenge him about?

9. What book follows 2 Chronicles in most modern Bibles?

10. Who requests wisdom in the first chapter of 2 Chronicles? (Hint: 1 Kings 3 contains a parallel account.)

# Answers to Bible Quiz 40: 1 and 2 Chronicles

1. The books of 1 and 2 Kings focus on the history of the northern kingdom (Israel) and the southern kingdom (Judah). The books of 1 and 2 Chronicles focus primarily on what nation: Israel, Judah, Egypt, or Assyria?   **Judah**

2. What is the first word of 1 Chronicles: *David*, *Adam*, *Seth*, or *The*?
   *Adam*

3. Who succeeds David as king at the end of 1 Chronicles?   **Solomon**

4. How many chapters are in 1 and 2 Chronicles combined: 55, 65, 75, or 85?   **65**

5. Chronicles was the last book of the Hebrew Old Testament.
   **True**

6. Who destroyed Jerusalem at the end of 2 Chronicles?
   **The Babylonians**

7. In the last three verses of 2 Chronicles, 70 years elapse and a decree is made. What is the decree?
   **The temple will be rebuilt, and the Jews may return to their land.**

8. In 2 Chronicles 26, King Uzziah becomes angry when challenged by 80 priests. What did they challenge him about?
   **He offered incense in the temple even though he was not a priest.**

9. What book follows 2 Chronicles in most modern Bibles?   **Ezra**

10. Who requests wisdom in the first chapter of 2 Chronicles? (Hint: 1 Kings 3 contains a parallel account.)
    **Solomon**

# Bible Quiz 41: Ezra and Nehemiah

1. In which of these two books is the wall around Jerusalem rebuilt?

2. In which book is the temple rebuilt?

3. Nehemiah was a priest. True or false?

4. Ezra was cupbearer to King Artaxerxes. True or false?

5. Sanballat was the Samaritan enemy of the builders. How many times is he mentioned in Nehemiah: 7, 10, 22, or 33?

6. During the exile, the Jews were unfaithful to God because they took wives from noncovenant people. Where is this recorded: Ezra, Nehemiah, neither, or both?

7. The wall around Jerusalem was completed in how much time: 1 day, 7 weeks, 52 days, or 70 years?

8. How long did Ezra read from the Book of the Law by the Water Gate: 1 hour, 3 hours, 6 hours, or 12 hours?

9. How many chapters are in Ezra and Nehemiah combined: 13, 23, 33, or 43?

10. In which century are these two books set?

# Answers to Bible Quiz 41: Ezra and Nehemiah

1. In which of these two books is the wall around Jerusalem rebuilt?

   **Nehemiah**

2. In which book is the temple rebuilt?

   **Ezra**

3. Nehemiah was a priest.

   **False**

4. Ezra was cupbearer to King Artaxerxes.

   **False**

5. Sanballat was the Samaritan enemy of the builders. How many times is he mentioned in Nehemiah: 7, 10, 22, or 33?

   **10**

6. During the exile, the Jews were unfaithful to God because they took wives from noncovenant people. Where is this recorded: Ezra, Nehemiah, neither, or both?

   **Both**

7. The wall around Jerusalem was completed in how much time: 1 day, 7 weeks, 52 days, or 70 years?

   **52 days**

8. How long did Ezra read from the Book of the Law by the Water Gate: 1 hour, 3 hours, 6 hours, or 12 hours?

   **6 hours**

9. How many chapters are in Ezra and Nehemiah combined: 13, 23, 33, or 43?

   **23**

10. In which century are these two books set?

    **The fifth century BC**

# Bible Quiz 42: Esther

1. Whom did Esther follow as queen?

2. What was Esther's Jewish (Hebrew) name?

3. Who was Esther's husband?

4. Where did he live: Susa, Ecbatana, Tehran, or Casiphia?

5. Who had adopted her and protected her all her life?

6. Who tried to kill this person and was eventually hanged on a gallows?

7. Which Jewish holiday derives from this fifth-century near-holocaust?

8. How many chapters does Esther have?

9. Which book follows Esther?

10. How did Esther save her people?

# Answers to Bible Quiz 42: Esther

1. Whom did Esther follow as queen?

   **Vashti**

2. What was Esther's Jewish (Hebrew) name?

   **Hadassah**

3. Who was Esther's husband?

   **Xerxes**

4. Where did he live: Susa, Ecbatana, Tehran, or Casiphia?

   **Susa**

5. Who had adopted her and protected her all her life?

   **Mordecai**

6. Who tried to kill this person and was eventually hanged on a gallows?

   **Haman**

7. Which Jewish holiday derives from this fifth-century near-holocaust?

   **Purim**

8. How many chapters does Esther have?

   **Ten**

9. Which book follows Esther?

   **Job**

10. How did Esther save her people?

    **She asked the king to stop the proposed genocide.**

# Bible Quiz 43: Job

1. Where did Job live: Israel, Uz, Egypt, or Anatolia?

2. Who are Eliphaz, Bildad, and Zophar?

3. Job called these men "miserable comforters" and "worthless
   _____."

4. Job lost all his close relations except for _____.

5. Who was apparently the youngest of the five primary human
   speakers in Job?

6. Whom did God allow to test and hurt Job?

7. Which Bible books mention Job? (Hint: The answer includes one
   Old Testament book besides Job and one New Testament book.)

8. Who rebukes Job from the storm?

9. Who was Jemimah?

10. What theological error does the book of Job refute?

# Answers to Bible Quiz 43: Job

1. Where did Job live: Israel, Uz, Egypt, or Anatolia?

    **Uz**

2. Who are Eliphaz, Bildad, and Zophar?

    **Job's friends**

3. Job called these men "miserable comforters" and "worthless
    _____."

    **Physicians**

4. Job lost all his close relations except for _____.

    **His wife**

5. Who was apparently the youngest of the five primary human
    speakers in Job?

    **Elihu**

6. Whom did God allow to test and hurt Job?

    **Satan**

7. Which Bible books mention Job? (Hint: The answer includes one
    Old Testament book besides Job and one New Testament book.)

    **Ezekiel and James**

8. Who rebukes Job from the storm?

    **God**

9. Who was Jemimah?

    **One of Job's daughters**

10. What theological error does the book of Job refute?

    **The misconception that people suffer only because of their
    specific sins**

# Bible Quiz 44: Psalms

1. How many psalms are included in the book of Psalms?

2. Psalms were originally intended to be accompanied by a percussion instrument. True or false?

3. Which book follows Psalms?

4. Psalm 151 is which of the following: nonexistent, apocryphal, canonical, or included in the New Testament?

5. Which psalm describes two ways and two kinds of people: 1, 19, 88, or 117?

6. In which psalm does the psalmist cry, "The darkness is my closest friend": 1, 19, 88, or 117?

7. Which psalm expresses a vision for all nations to come to know God: 1, 19, 88, or 117?

8. Which psalm extols the wonders of the word of God: 1, 19, 88, or 117?

9. Which psalm is the longest acrostic psalm in the psalter?

10. Which of these is *not* considered one of the "sin psalms": 32, 38, 51, or 118?

# Answers to Bible Quiz 44: Psalms

1. How many psalms are included in the book of Psalms? **150**

2. Psalms were originally intended to be accompanied by a percussion instrument.

   **False. Many were to be sung with stringed instruments.**

3. Which book follows Psalms? **Proverbs**

4. Psalm 151 is which of the following: nonexistent, apocryphal, canonical, or included in the New Testament?

   **Apocryphal. It does not properly belong in the canon, but it does occasionally appear in some Bibles.**

5. Which psalm describes two ways and two kinds of people: 1, 19, 88, or 117?

   **1**

6. In which psalm does the psalmist cry, "The darkness is my closest friend": 1, 19, 88, or 117?

   **88**

7. Which psalm expresses a vision for all nations to come to know God: 1, 19, 88, or 117?

   **117**

8. Which psalm extols the wonders of the word of God: 1, 19, 88, or 117?

   **19**

9. Which psalm is the longest acrostic psalm in the psalter? **119**

10. Which of these is *not* considered one of the "sin psalms": 32, 38, 51, or 118?

    **118**

# Bible Quiz 45: Proverbs

1. Who is credited with writing most of the Proverbs?

2. Which three chapters deal with avoiding the adulteress: 1–3, 5–7, 15–17, or 21–23?

3. In which chapter does the woman of noble character appear?

4. In which chapter do we read that good news from a distant land is like cool water to the soul?

5. "The guilty flee when none pursue" is found in which chapter: 8, 18, 28, or 38?

6. "The fear of the LORD is the beginning of _____."

7. "As _____ sharpens _____, so one man sharpens another."

8. "Do not add to his words, or he will rebuke you and prove you a liar" is found in what verse: 10:6; 20:6; 30:6; or 33:6?

9. Which book follows Proverbs?

10. "He who spares the rod _____ his son" (Proverbs 13:24).

# Answers to Bible Quiz 45: Proverbs

1. Who is credited with writing most of the Proverbs?

    **Solomon**

2. Which three chapters deal with avoiding the adulteress: 1–3, 5–7, 15–17, or 21–23?

    **5–7**

3. In which chapter does the woman of noble character appear?

    **31**

4. Where do we read that good news from a distant land is like cool water to the soul?

    **25**

5. "The guilty flee when none pursue" is found in which chapter: 8, 18, 28, or 38?

    **28**

6. "The fear of the LORD is the beginning of _____."

    **Knowledge (1:7) or wisdom (9:10)**

7. "As _____ sharpens _____, so one man sharpens another."

    **Iron**

8. "Do not add to his words, or he will rebuke you and prove you a liar" is found in what verse: 10:6; 20:6; 30:6; or 33:6?

    **30:6**

9. Which book follows Proverbs?

    **Ecclesiastes**

10. "He who spares the rod _____ his son" (Proverbs 13:24).

    **Hates**

# Bible Quiz 46: Ecclesiastes

1. To whom is this book attributed?

2. Ecclesiastes has 14 chapters. True or false?

3. Which book follows Ecclesiastes?

4. "There is a time for everything, and a season for every activity under heaven." This famous poem is found in chapter _____.

5. "Whoever loves wealth is never satisfied with _____" (Ecclesiastes 5:10).

6. "There is not a righteous man on earth who does what is right and never sins." This is called "the Romans 3:23 of the Old Testament" and is found in what verse: 1:5; 4:4; 7:20; or 12:14?

7. "If a man is _____, the rafters sag" (Ecclesiastes 10:18).

8. "Now all has been heard; here is the conclusion of the matter: Fear God and keep his commandments, for this is the whole duty of man. For God will bring every deed into judgment, including every hidden thing, whether it is good or evil." This passage appears in the middle chapter of Ecclesiastes. True or false?

9. Who was the father of the Teacher?

10. Life "under the sun" (without God) is _____.

## Answers to Bible Quiz 46: Ecclesiastes

1. To whom is this book attributed?   **Solomon**

2. Ecclesiastes has 14 chapters.
   **False. It has 12 chapters.**

3. Which book follows Ecclesiastes?   **Song of Songs**

4. "There is a time for everything, and a season for every activity under heaven." This famous poem is found in chapter _____.
   **3**

5. "Whoever loves wealth is never satisfied with _____" (Ecclesiastes 5:10).
   **His income**

6. "There is not a righteous man on earth who does what is right and never sins." This is called "the Romans 3:23 of the Old Testament" and is found in what verse: 1:5; 4:4; 7:20; or 12:14?
   **7:20**

7. "If a man is _____, the rafters sag" (Ecclesiastes 10:18).
   **Lazy**

8. "Now all has been heard; here is the conclusion of the matter: Fear God and keep his commandments, for this is the whole duty of man. For God will bring every deed into judgment, including every hidden thing, whether it is good or evil." This passage appears in the middle chapter of Ecclesiastes.
   **False. It is the final passage of the book.**

9. Who was the father of the Teacher?   **David**

10. Life "under the sun" (without God) is _____.
    **Meaningless, empty, vanity, or futile**

# Bible Quiz 47: Song of Songs

1. Who does the groom appear to be in Song of Songs?

2. In which city is Song of Songs set?

3. How is the bride addressed: Shunnamite, Shulamith, Shibboleth, Shulammite?

4. In chapter 2, we read the admonition, "Catch for us the _____."

5. Which book of the Bible follows Song of Songs?

6. What is another name for this book: Canticles, Lovesick, Ode to Love, or Lamentations?

7. "Many waters cannot _____; rivers cannot wash it away" (Song of Songs 8:7).

- stop romance
- quench love
- extinguish passion
- forgive sin

8. This is one refrain in the book: "Do not arouse or awaken love until it so desires." Which of these is a fitting modern-day way of saying this?

- Let her sleep.
- True love waits.
- Obey your thirst.
- Love deeply.

9. The final passage of the book reads,

- "Come away, my lover, and be like a gazelle or like a young stag on the spice-laden mountains."
- "His left arm is under my head and his right arm embraces me."
- "His arms are rods of gold set with chrysolite. His body is like polished ivory decorated with sapphires."
- "I am a rose of Sharon, a lily of the valleys."

10. How many chapters are in Song of Songs: 4, 8, 12, or 16?

# Answers to Bible Quiz 47: Song of Songs

1. Who does the groom appear to be in Song of Songs?

   **Solomon**

2. In which city is Song of Songs set?

   **Jerusalem**

3. How is the bride addressed: Shunnamite, Shulamith, Shibboleth, Shulammite?

   **Shulammite or Shulamith**

4. In chapter 2, we read the admonition, "Catch for us the _____."

   **Foxes or jackals**

5. Which book of the Bible follows Song of Songs?

   **Isaiah**

6. What is another name for this book: Canticles, Lovesick, Ode to Love, or Lamentations?

   **Canticles**

7. "Many waters cannot _____; rivers cannot wash it away" (Song of Songs 8:7).

   **Quench love**

8. This is one refrain in the book: "Do not arouse or awaken love until it so desires." Which of these is a fitting modern-day way of saying this?

   **True love waits**

9. The final passage of the book reads,

   **"Come away, my lover, and be like a gazelle or like a young stag on the spice-laden mountains."**

10. How many chapters are in Song of Songs: 4, 8, 12, or 16?  **8**

# Bible Quiz 48: Isaiah

1. During which century before Christ did Isaiah minister: the tenth, eighth, fifth, or second?

2. How many chapters are in this relatively long book of the Bible: 44, 55, 66, 77, or 88?

3. "Come now, let us reason together" appears in which chapter?

4. What event in Isaiah's life takes place in chapter 6?

5. Whom do Isaiah's "servant songs" ultimately refer to?

6. Which book precedes Isaiah?

7. Chapter 5 contains a parable. What is the subject?

   - the prodigal son
   - the lost coins
   - the vineyard
   - the selfish shepherd

8. Isaiah warns the unrepentant of the certainty of exile. But he also offers hope that _____ will take place afterward.

   - heaven
   - return from captivity
   - showers of blessing
   - righteous sacrifices

9. Which other prophet lived and prophesied at about the same time as Isaiah: Jeremiah, Amos, Elijah, or Habakkuk?

10. Which Gentile ruler is prophesied by name in chapter 44?

# Answers to Bible Quiz 48: Isaiah

1. During which century before Christ did Isaiah minister: the tenth, eighth, fifth, or second?

   **Eighth**

2. How many chapters are in this relatively long book of the Bible: 44, 55, 66, 77, or 88?

   **66**

3. "Come now, let us reason together" appears in which chapter?

   **1**

4. What event in Isaiah's life takes place in chapter 6?

   **His call to be a prophet**

5. Whom do Isaiah's "servant songs" ultimately refer to?

   **Jesus Christ**

6. Which book precedes Isaiah?

   **Song of Songs**

7. Chapter 5 contains a parable. What is the subject?

   **The vineyard**

8. Isaiah warns the unrepentant of the certainty of exile. But he also offers hope that _____ will take place afterward.

   **Return from captivity**

9. Which other prophet lived and prophesied at about the same time as Isaiah: Jeremiah, Amos, Elijah, or Habakkuk?

   **Amos**

10. Which Gentile ruler is referred to prophetically by name in chapter 44?

    **Cyrus**

# Bible Quiz 49: Jeremiah and Lamentations

1. Jeremiah is the "before" and Lamentations is the "after." True or false?

2. These books together have 57 chapters in all. True or false?

3. What is the name of Jeremiah's secretary? (His personal seal was recently identified by an archaeologist!)

4. Who cut slices off of Jeremiah's message and threw them into the fire (chapter 36): Saul, Uzziah, Jehoiakim, or David?

5. To which devastated and deserted city does Lamentations 1 refer?

6. "The steadfast love of the LORD never ceases" (RSV). This sentence appears in which book, Jeremiah or in Lamentations?

7. When did Jeremiah minister?
   - 1010–970 BC
   - 626–586 BC
   - 433–393 BC
   - 30 BC–AD 11

8. The prophecy of the new covenant appears in which chapter of Jeremiah: 11, 31, 41, or 61?

9. In chapter 20, Jeremiah curses the day of his birth. True or false?

10. "The heart is deceitful" appears in Jeremiah 19:7. True or false?

# Answers to Bible Quiz 49: Jeremiah and Lamentations

1. Jeremiah is the "before" and Lamentations is the "after."   **True**

2. These books together have 57 chapters in all.
   **True**

3. What is the name of Jeremiah's secretary? (His personal seal was recently identified by an archaeologist!)   **Baruch**

4. Who cut slices off of Jeremiah's message and threw them into the fire (chapter 36): Saul, Uzziah, Jehoiakim, or David?
   **Jehoiakim**

5. To which devastated and deserted city does Lamentations 1 refer?
   **Jerusalem**

6. "The steadfast love of the LORD never ceases" (RSV). This sentence appears in which book, Jeremiah or in Lamentations?
   **Lamentations**

7. When did Jeremiah minister?
   **626–586 BC**

8. The prophecy of the new covenant appears in which chapter of Jeremiah: 11, 31, 41, or 61?
   **31**

9. In chapter 20, Jeremiah curses the day of his birth.
   **True**

10. "The heart is deceitful" appears in Jeremiah 19:7.
   **False. The correct reference is 17:9.**

# Bible Quiz 50: Ezekiel

1. Which book of the Bible comes right before Ezekiel?

2. Ezekiel refers to the Good Shepherd in which chapter: 24, 34, 44, or 54?

3. When did Ezekiel live: the 900s BC, 500s BC, 300s BC, or 100s BC?

4. Gog and Magog, unspecified enemies of the people of God, are mentioned in the book of Ezekiel. True or false?

5. The vision of the dry bones appears in Ezekiel 37. True or false?

6. The allegory of unfaithful Jerusalem appears in Ezekiel 16. True or false?

7. Chapters 3 and 33 both contain passages about the watchman. What musical instrument was the watchman supposed to sound to alert the people of the approaching enemy?

8. Which book immediately follows Ezekiel?

9. Who is mentioned in the closing chapters of Ezekiel: the Antichrist, the Hatchet Man, the prince, or the princess?

10. Ezekiel denounced all these evil practices except which one: idolatry, heliolatry (sun worship), sacrificing to the Queen of Heaven, or whitewashing sin?

# Answers to Bible Quiz 50: Ezekiel

1. Which book of the Bible comes right before Ezekiel?
   **Lamentations**

2. Ezekiel refers to the Good Shepherd in which chapter: 24, 34, 44, or 54?
   **34**

3. When did Ezekiel live: the 900s BC, 500s BC, 300s BC, or 100s BC?
   **500s BC**

4. Gog and Magog, unspecified enemies of the people of God, are mentioned in the book of Ezekiel.   **True**

5. The vision of the dry bones appears in Ezekiel 37.   **True**

6. The allegory of unfaithful Jerusalem appears in Ezekiel 16.   **True**

7. Chapters 3 and 33 both contain passages about the watchman. What musical instrument was the watchman supposed to sound to alert the people of the approaching enemy?   **Trumpet**

8. Which book immediately follows Ezekiel?   **Daniel**

9. Who is mentioned in the closing chapters of Ezekiel: the Antichrist, the Hatchet Man, the prince, or the princess?   **The prince**

10. Ezekiel denounced all these evil practices except which one: idolatry, heliolatry (sun worship), sacrificing to the Queen of Heaven, or whitewashing sin?
    **Sacrificing to the Queen of Heaven**

# Bible Quiz 51: Daniel

1. The Ancient of Days is mentioned in which chapter of Daniel: 1, 2, 7, or 12?

2. The resurrection is mentioned in which chapter of Daniel: 1, 2, 7, or 12?

3. Nebuchadnezzar's dream is explained in which chapter of Daniel: 1, 2, 7, or 12?

4. Daniel refuses to eat unclean food in which chapter: 1, 2, 7, or 12?

5. How many chapters are in Daniel?

6. Which languages is the book written in?

7. Which biblical book follows Daniel?

8. Daniel was thrown into a blazing furnace. True or false?

9. Daniel was thrown into the lions' den. True or false?

10. What was written on the wall before Belshazzar's eyes (chapter 5)?
    - *Eloi Eloi lama sabachthani*
    - *Talitha koum*
    - *Marana tha*
    - *Mene mene tekel parsin*
    - *Maher Shalal Hash Baz*

# Answers to Bible Quiz 51: Daniel

1. The Ancient of Days is mentioned in which chapter of Daniel: 1, 2, 7, or 12?

    **7**

2. The resurrection is mentioned in which chapter of Daniel: 1, 2, 7, or 12?

    **12**

3. Nebuchadnezzar's dream is explained in which chapter of Daniel: 1, 2, 7, or 12?

    **2**

4. Daniel refuses to eat unclean food in which chapter: 1, 2, 7, or 12?

    **1**

5. How many chapters are in Daniel?

    **12**

6. Which languages is the book written in?

    **Hebrew and Aramaic**

7. Which biblical book follows Daniel?

    **Hosea**

8. Daniel was thrown into a blazing furnace.

    **False**

9. Daniel was thrown into the lions' den.

    **True**

10. What was written on the wall before Belshazzar's eyes (chapter 5)?

    *Mene mene tekel parsin*

# Bible Quiz 52: Hosea

1. What event in Hosea's personal life is a picture of the spiritual life of Israel?

2. Who (presumably) wrote Hosea?

3. Who was Hosea's unfaithful wife?

4. How many chapters are in Hosea: 8, 14, 20, or 22?

5. Which book follows Hosea?

6. Hosea prophesied during the reigns of Uzziah, Jotham, Ahaz, and Hezekiah in the sixth century BC. True or false?

7. Who were Jezreel, Lo-Ruhamah, and Lo-Ammi?

8. "I desire mercy, not sacrifice, and acknowledgment of God rather than burnt offerings" (Hosea 6:6). Who quoted this twice in the book of Matthew?

9. *Hoshea* is another form of *Yeshua* (Jesus' name). What does *Hoshea* mean?

10. Hosea is the first of the minor prophets. How many more are there?

## Answers to Bible Quiz 52: Hosea

1. What event in Hosea's personal life is a picture of the spiritual life of Israel?

   **Adultery**

2. Who (presumably) wrote Hosea?

   **Hosea**

3. Who was Hosea's unfaithful wife?

   **Gomer**

4. How many chapters are in Hosea: 8, 14, 20, or 22?

   **14**

5. Which book follows Hosea?

   **Joel**

6. Hosea prophesied during the reigns of Uzziah, Jotham, Ahaz, and Hezekiah in the sixth century BC.

   **False. Those are the right kings, but he ministered in the eighth century BC.**

7. Who were Jezreel, Lo-Ruhamah, and Lo-Ammi?

   **Children of Hosea and Gomer**

8. "I desire mercy, not sacrifice, and acknowledgment of God rather than burnt offerings" (Hosea 6:6). Who quoted this twice in the book of Matthew?

   **Jesus**

9. *Hoshea* is another form of *Yeshua* (Jesus' name). What does *Hoshea* mean?

   **Salvation**

10. Hosea is the first of the minor prophets. How many more are there?

   **11**

# Bible Quiz 53: Joel

1. Joel compares an invading foreign army to what animals: spiders, ants, locusts, or scorpions?

2. The sixth-century invader Joel refers to is Babylon. True or false?

3. How many chapters are in Joel?

4. Which other minor prophets have this same number of chapters?

5. Peter quotes from Joel 2 in Acts chapter _____.

6. Joel was the son of Pethuel. True or false?

7. Joel 3:10, reversing Isaiah 2:4, reads "Beat your plowshares into swords and your pruning hooks into _____. Let the weakling say, 'I am strong!'"

8. "Multitudes, multitudes in the valley of _____" (Joel 3:14).
   - the shadow of death
   - the dolls
   - decision
   - the dinosaurs

9. What book comes just before Joel?

10. "A nation has invaded my land, powerful and without number; it has the teeth of a lion, the fangs of a _____" (1:6).

# Answers to Bible Quiz 53: Joel

1. Joel compares an invading foreign army to what animals: spiders, ants, locusts, or scorpions?

   **Locusts**

2. The sixth-century invader Joel refers to is Babylon.

   **True**

3. How many chapters are in Joel?

   **Three**

4. Which other minor prophets have this same number of chapters?

   **Nahum, Habakkuk, and Zephaniah**

5. Peter quotes from Joel 2 in Acts chapter _____.

   **2**

6. Joel was the son of Pethuel.

   **True**

7. Joel 3:10, reversing Isaiah 2:4, reads "Beat your plowshares into swords and your pruning hooks into _____. Let the weakling say, 'I am strong!'"

   **Spears**

8. "Multitudes, multitudes in the valley of _____" (Joel 3:14).

   **Decision**

9. What book comes just before Joel?

   **Hosea**

10. "A nation has invaded my land, powerful and without number; it has the teeth of a lion, the fangs of a _____" (1:6).

    **Lioness**

# Bible Quiz 54: Amos

1. What was one of Amos's two professions before becoming a prophet?

2. What was his other profession?

3. Amos prophesied during the reign of Uzziah, king of Judah. Who was the king of Israel: Jeroboam II, Solomon, Zedekiah, or Ahab?

4. The crescendo of judgment in chapters 1–2 begins with prophecies against Damascus, Gaza, Tyre, Edom, Ammon, and Moab. What was one of the other two nations named in the list?

5. What was the other nation named in the list?

6. Amos has 11 chapters. True or false?

7. Amos 5:21 reads, "I hate, I despise your religious feasts; I cannot stand your _____."

8. The famous Amos 5:24 reads, "But let _____ roll on like a river, righteousness like a never-failing stream!"

9. What is the book following Amos—and the subject of the next quiz?

10. The encouraging words of 9:13 are, "'The days are coming,' declares the LORD, 'when the _____ will be overtaken by the plowman and the planter by the one treading grapes.'"

# Answers to Bible Quiz 54: Amos

1. What was one of Amos's two professions before becoming a prophet?

   **Shepherd**

2. What was his other profession?    **Dresser of sycamore-fig trees**

3. Amos prophesied during the reign of Uzziah, king of Judah. Who was the king of Israel: Jeroboam II, Solomon, Zedekiah, or Ahab?

   **Jeroboam II**

4. The crescendo of judgment in chapters 1–2 begins with prophecies against Damascus, Gaza, Tyre, Edom, Ammon, and Moab. What was one of the other two nations named in the list?

   **Judah**

5. What was the other nation named in the list?    **Israel**

6. Amos has 11 chapters.

   **False. It has nine.**

7. Amos 5:21 reads, "I hate, I despise your religious feasts; I cannot stand your _____."

   **Religious assemblies**

8. The famous Amos 5:24 reads, "But let _____ roll on like a river, righteousness like a never-failing stream!"

   **Justice**

9. What is the book following Amos—and the subject of the next quiz?

   **Obadiah**

10. The encouraging words of 9:13 are, "'The days are coming,' declares the LORD, 'when the _____ will be overtaken by the plowman and the planter by the one treading grapes.'"

    **Reaper**

# Bible Quiz 55: Obadiah

1. How many chapters are in Obadiah?

2. How many other books in the Bible have the same number of chapters?

3. Obadiah means "servant of Yah[weh]." True or false?

4. According to 1:1, the oracle is about which nation? (Hint: 1:6 reads, "But how Esau will be ransacked, his hidden treasures pillaged!")

5. Lamenting the deplorable behavior of this same nation on the day Babylon destroyed Zion, the Lord said through Obadiah, "On the day you stood aloof while strangers carried off his wealth and foreigners entered his gates and cast lots for Jerusalem, you were _____."

6. Which book follows Obadiah?

7. Which book precedes Obadiah?

8. Which of these summarizes Obadiah the best:

   - enemies versus friends
   - holiness versus ungodliness
   - revenge versus forgiveness
   - looking down versus looking up

9. This book is quoted twice in the New Testament. True or false?

10. The final verse of the book is, "Deliverers will go up on Mount Zion to govern the mountains of Esau. And the kingdom will be _____."

# Answers to Bible Quiz 55: Obadiah

1. How many chapters are in Obadiah?    **One**

2. How many other books in the Bible have the same number of chapters?
   **Four: Philemon, 2 John, 3 John, and Jude**

3. Obadiah means "servant of Yah[weh]."    **True**

4. According to 1:1, the oracle is about which nation? (Hint: 1:6 reads, "But how Esau will be ransacked, his hidden treasures pillaged!")
   **Edom**

5. Lamenting the deplorable behavior of this same nation on the day Babylon destroyed Zion, the Lord said through Obadiah, "On the day you stood aloof while strangers carried off his wealth and foreigners entered his gates and cast lots for Jerusalem, you were _____."
   **Like one of them**

6. Which book follows Obadiah?    **Jonah**

7. Which book precedes Obadiah?    **Amos**

8. Which of these summarizes Obadiah the best?
   **Revenge versus forgiveness**

9. This book is quoted twice in the New Testament.
   **False**

10. The final verse of the book is, "Deliverers will go up on Mount Zion to govern the mountains of Esau. And the kingdom will be _____."
    **The Lord's**

# Bible Quiz 56: Jonah

1. To which nation was Jonah sent to preach: Assyria, Babylon, Persia, or Greece?

2. How many chapters are in Jonah?

3. What did Jonah do when he boarded the ship bound for Tarshish?

4. What did the sailors do to Jonah because of his repeated insistence?

5. What did Jonah do while in the interior of the large animal that swallowed him?

6. Why did Jonah run from the mission on which the Lord had sent him?

7. Jonah warned that Nineveh would be destroyed in _____ days.

8. The king of Nineveh failed to repent. True or false?

9. Jonah wanted the Ninevites to be destroyed. True or false?

10. What was apparently the population of Nineveh: 1200, 12,000, 120,000, or 1,200,000?

# Answers to Bible Quiz 56: Jonah

1. To which nation was Jonah sent to preach: Assyria, Babylon, Persia, or Greece?

   **Assyria**

2. How many chapters are in Jonah?

   **Four**

3. What did Jonah do when he boarded the ship bound for Tarshish?

   **He fell asleep.**

4. What did the sailors do to Jonah because of his repeated insistence?

   **They threw him overboard.**

5. What did Jonah do while in the interior of the large animal that swallowed him?

   **He prayed.**

6. Why did Jonah run from the mission on which the Lord had sent him?

   **Prejudice. He did not want God to forgive the Ninevites.**

7. Jonah warned that Nineveh would be destroyed in _____ days.

   **40**

8. The king of Nineveh failed to repent.

   **False**

9. Jonah wanted the Ninevites to be destroyed.

   **True**

10. What was apparently the population of Nineveh: 1200, 12,000, 120,000, or 1,200,000?

    **120,000**

# Bible Quiz 57: Micah

1. Micah spoke in the 600s BC, shortly before the invasion of the Babylonians. True or false?

2. In which chapter is the birthplace of the Messiah prophesied?

3. Micah engages the service of an idolatrous priest in the book of Judges. True or false?

4. Micah prophesied concerning Samaria and _____ (Micah 1:1).

5. Micah 6:8 reads, "He has showed you, O man, what is good. And what does the LORD require of you? To act justly and to love mercy and to _____ with your God."

   - walk humbly
   - commune in silence
   - compromise commitment
   - speak reverently

6. Which book follows Micah?

7. Micah 4:1 reads, "In the last days the mountain of the LORD's temple will be established as chief among the mountains; it will be raised above the hills, and _____."

   - peoples will stream to it
   - great will be the power of the Almighty
   - yea, even the hillbillies shall come thereto

8. How many chapters are in Micah: one, three, five, seven, or nine?

9. According to Jeremiah 26:18, Micah of Moresheth prophesied during whose reign: Hezekiah, Saul, Zedekiah, or Manasseh?

10. In Micah 1:4, what happens when the Lord comes down from his dwelling places and treads the high places of the earth?

    - the mountains melt
    - the valleys split apart
    - neither A nor B
    - both A and B

# Answers to Bible Quiz 57: Micah

1. Micah spoke in the 600s BC, shortly before the invasion of the Babylonians.

   **False. Micah ministered many years before the Babylonian invasion.**

2. In which chapter is the birthplace of the Messiah prophesied?   **5**

3. Micah engages the service of an idolatrous priest in the book of Judges.   **True. But this is a different Micah.**

4. Micah prophesied concerning Samaria and _____ (Micah 1:1).

   **Jerusalem**

5. Micah 6:8 reads, "He has showed you, O man, what is good. And what does the LORD require of you? To act justly and to love mercy and to _____with your God."   **Walk humbly**

6. Which book follows Micah?   **Nahum**

7. Micah 4:1 reads, "In the last days the mountain of the LORD's temple will be established as chief among the mountains; it will be raised above the hills, and _____."

   **Peoples will stream to it.**

8. How many chapters are in Micah: one, three, five, seven, or nine?

   **Seven**

9. According to Jeremiah 26:18, Micah of Moresheth prophesied during whose reign: Hezekiah, Saul, Zedekiah, or Manasseh?

   **Hezekiah**

10. In Micah 1:4, what happens when the Lord comes down from his dwelling places and treads the high places of the earth?

    **Both A and B: The mountains melt, and the valleys split apart.**

# Bible Quiz 58: Nahum and Habakkuk

1. Nahum prophesied concerning which nation: Nineveh, Nimrud, Nanjing, or Nantucket?

2. Habakkuk prophesied concerning which nation: Judah, Israel, Egypt, or Moab?

3. Nahum has three chapters. True or false?

4. Habakkuk has three chapters. True or false?

5. "Nothing can heal your wound; your injury is fatal. Everyone who hears the news about you claps his hands at your fall, for who has not felt your endless cruelty?" Are these words the final verse of Nahum or of Habakkuk?

6. "Though the fig tree does not bud and there are no grapes on the vines, though the olive crop fails and the fields produce no food, though there are no sheep in the pen and no cattle in the stalls, yet I will rejoice in the LORD, I will be joyful in God my Savior. The Sovereign LORD is my strength; he makes my feet like the feet of a deer, he enables me to go on the heights." Are these words the final verses of Nahum or of Habakkuk?

7. Which book precedes Nahum?

8. Which book follows Habakkuk?

9. Which prophet questions God about his justice?

10. Which prophet does Paul quote in Romans when he writes, "He who by faith is righteous shall live," or "The righteous will live by faith"?

# Answers to Bible Quiz 58: Nahum and Habakkuk

1. Nahum prophesied concerning which nation: Nineveh, Nimrud, Nanjing, or Nantucket?   **Nineveh**

2. Habakkuk prophesied concerning which nation: Judah, Israel, Egypt, or Moab?   **Judah**

3. Nahum has three chapters.   **True**

4. Habakkuk has three chapters.   **True**

5. "Nothing can heal your wound; your injury is fatal. Everyone who hears the news about you claps his hands at your fall, for who has not felt your endless cruelty?" Are these words the final verse of Nahum or of Habakkuk?   **Nahum**

6. "Though the fig tree does not bud and there are no grapes on the vines, though the olive crop fails and the fields produce no food, though there are no sheep in the pen and no cattle in the stalls, yet I will rejoice in the LORD, I will be joyful in God my Savior. The Sovereign LORD is my strength; he makes my feet like the feet of a deer, he enables me to go on the heights." Are these words the final verses of Nahum or of Habakkuk?   **Habakkuk**

7. Which book precedes Nahum?   **Micah**

8. Which book follows Habakkuk?   **Zephaniah**

9. Which prophet questions God about his justice?   **Habakkuk**

10. Which prophet does Paul quote in Romans when he writes, "He who by faith is righteous shall live," or "The righteous will live by faith"?   **Habakkuk**

# Bible Quiz 59: Zephaniah and Haggai

1. Which of these two books is longer?

2. How many chapters does the shorter of the two contain?

3. The longer one contains 14 chapters. True or false?

4. Zephaniah's message came during the time of King Josiah. Approximately when was that?

   - 780–770 BC
   - 710–700 BC
   - 660–650 BC
   - 620–610 BC

5. Haggai's message came in the time of King Darius of Persia. Approximately when was that?

   - 700–690 BC
   - 600–590 BC
   - 520–510 BC
   - 440–430 BC

6. What prophet helped Haggai challenge the Jews to rebuild the temple?

7. The challenge to rebuild the temple came after the time of Nehemiah. True or false?

8. Which book follows Haggai?

9. Zephaniah 1:5 refers to Judah's worship of Baal and Molech. True or false?

10. Which prophet said, "Is it a time for you yourselves to be living in your paneled houses, while this house remains a ruin?"

# Answers to Bible Quiz 59: Zephaniah and Haggai

1. Which of these two books is longer?

   **Zephaniah**

2. How many chapters does the shorter of the two contain?

   **Two**

3. The longer one contains 14 chapters.

   **False**

4. Zephaniah's message came during the time of King Josiah. Approximately when was that?

   **620–610 BC**

5. Haggai's message came in the time of King Darius of Persia. Approximately when was that?

   **520–510 BC**

6. What prophet helped Haggai challenge the Jews to rebuild the temple?

   **Zechariah**

7. The challenge to rebuild the temple came after the time of Nehemiah.

   **False**

8. Which book follows Haggai?

   **Zechariah**

9. Zephaniah 1:5 refers to Judah's worship of Baal and Molech.

   **True**

10. Which prophet said, "Is it a time for you yourselves to be living in your paneled houses, while this house remains a ruin?"

    **Haggai (1:4)**

# Bible Quiz 60: Zechariah and Malachi

1. Malachi is the last book of the English Bible. True or false?

2. Malachi is the last book of the Hebrew Bible. True or false?

3. Malachi wrote in the 400s BC. True or false?

4. Zechariah wrote in the 500s BC. True or false?

5. Who was Zechariah's partner in preaching, prophesying, and motivating the people of God to rebuild the temple?

6. Which book foretells the coming of John the Baptist?

7. In which book does God say, "I hate divorce"?

8. Which book contains more messianic prophecy (by far)?

9. How many books of the Bible start with the letter Z?

10. Which book of the Bible is Zechariah: thirty-eighth, fortieth, forty-third, or forty-fifth?

# Answers to Bible Quiz 60: Zechariah and Malachi

1. Malachi is the last book of the English Bible.
   **False. Revelation is the last book.**

2. Malachi is the last book of the Hebrew Bible.
   **False. Chronicles is the last book.**

3. Malachi wrote in the 400s BC.
   **True**

4. Zechariah wrote in the 500s BC.
   **True**

5. Who was Zechariah's partner in preaching, prophesying, and motivating the people of God to rebuild the temple?
   **Haggai**

6. Which book foretells the coming of John the Baptist?
   **Malachi**

7. In which book does God say, "I hate divorce"?
   **Malachi**

8. Which book contains more messianic prophecy (by far)?
   **Zechariah**

9. How many books of the Bible start with the letter *Z*?
   **Two: Zephaniah and Zechariah**

10. Which book of the Bible is Zechariah: thirty-eighth, fortieth, forty-third, or forty-fifth?
    **Thirty-eighth**

# Bible Quiz 61: The Gospel of Matthew

1. The Sermon on the Mount is found in Matthew. True or false?

2. The Great Commission is found in Matthew. True or false?

3. The Greatest Commandment is found in Matthew and Mark, but not in Luke. True or false?

4. The Golden Rule is found in Matthew. True or false?

5. What does Matthew place at the beginning of his Gospel: Jesus' genealogy, Jesus' baptism, the resurrection, or the sermon in Nazareth?

6. Matthew has 28 chapters. True or false?

7. Where is Matthew's conversion found: 9:9; 10:10; 11:11; or 12:12?

8. The book immediately before Matthew is Malachi. True or false?

9. The parable of the sheep and the goats does not appear in Matthew. True or false?

10. Which chapter of Matthew is rich in parables: 13, 14, 15, 16?

# Answers to Bible Quiz 61: The Gospel of Matthew

1. The Sermon on the Mount is found in Matthew.
   **True**

2. The Great Commission is found in Matthew.
   **True**

3. The Greatest Commandment is found in Matthew and Mark, but not in Luke.
   **False. It is included in all three.**

4. The Golden Rule is found in Matthew.
   **True**

5. What does Matthew place at the beginning of his Gospel: Jesus' genealogy, Jesus' baptism, the resurrection, or the sermon in Nazareth?
   **Jesus' genealogy**

6. Matthew has 28 chapters.
   **True**

7. Where is Matthew's conversion found: 9:9; 10:10; 11:11; or 12:12?
   **9:9**

8. The book immediately before Matthew is Malachi.
   **True**

9. The parable of the sheep and the goats does not appear in Matthew.
   **False**

10. Which chapter of Matthew is rich in parables: 13, 14, 15, 16?
    **13**

# Bible Quiz 62: The Gospel of Mark

1. Mark is the shortest of the four Gospels. True or false?

2. The crucifixion is recounted in Mark 15. True or false?

3. The authenticity of the ending of Mark's Gospel is uncertain. True or false?

4. "Very early in the morning, while it was still dark, Jesus got up, left the house and went off to a solitary place, where he _____" (Mark 1:35).

5. Mark's Gospel begins, "In the beginning was the Word." True or false?

6. Jesus predicts the Roman destruction of Jerusalem in chapter 13. True or false?

7. Mark is the forty-first book of the Bible. True or false?

8. "Then he called the crowd to him along with his disciples and said: 'If anyone would come after me, he must deny himself and take up his cross and follow me.'" What chapter is this verse in: 8, 13, 16, or none of the those?

9. The dance of Herodias's daughter, which led to John the Baptist's decapitation, is recounted in Matthew, Mark, and Luke. True or false?

10. The Gerasene demoniac is exorcised in chapter 5. True or false?

# Answers to Bible Quiz 62: The Gospel of Mark

1. Mark is the shortest of the four Gospels.
   **True**

2. The crucifixion is recounted in Mark 15.
   **True**

3. The authenticity of the ending of Mark's Gospel is uncertain.   **True**

4. "Very early in the morning, while it was still dark, Jesus got up, left the house and went off to a solitary place, where he _____" (Mark 1:35).   **Prayed**

5. Mark's Gospel begins, "In the beginning was the Word."   **False**

6. Jesus predicts the Roman destruction of Jerusalem in chapter 13.   **True**

7. Mark is the forty-first book of the Bible.
   **True**

8. "Then he called the crowd to him along with his disciples and said: 'If anyone would come after me, he must deny himself and take up his cross and follow me.'" What chapter is this verse in: 8, 13, 16, or none of the those?   **8**

9. The dance of Herodias's daughter, which led to John the Baptist's decapitation, is recounted in Matthew, Mark, and Luke.
   **False. It is recorded in Matthew and Mark, but not in Luke.**

10. The Gerasene demoniac is exorcised in chapter 5.   **True**

# Bible Quiz 63: The Gospel of Luke

1. Luke contains the most text of the four Gospels. True or false?

2. What is the sequel to Luke?

3. What was Luke's profession?

4. The Emmaus Road incident appears only in Luke. True or false?

5. Which book immediately follows Luke?

6. Who was the high priest and son-in-law of Annas?

7. The resurrection occurs in what chapter of Luke: 21, 22, 23, or 24?

8. The Sermon on the Plain is found in Luke 6. True or false?

9. In Luke 13, Jesus calls Herod Antipas a _____.

10. The thief on the cross is pardoned only in Luke's Gospel. True or false?

# Answers to Bible Quiz 63: The Gospel of Luke

1. Luke contains the most text of the four Gospels.

   **True**

2. What is the sequel to Luke?

   **Acts**

3. What was Luke's profession?

   **He was a physician.**

4. The Emmaus Road incident appears only in Luke.

   **True**

5. Which book immediately follows Luke?

   **John**

6. Who was the high priest and son-in-law of Annas?

   **Caiaphas**

7. The resurrection occurs in what chapter of Luke: 21, 22, 23, or 24?

   **24**

8. The Sermon on the Plain is found in Luke 6.

   **True**

9. In Luke 13, Jesus calls Herod Antipas a _____.

   **Fox**

10. The thief on the cross is pardoned only in Luke's Gospel.

    **True**

# Bible Quiz 64: The Gospel of John

1. Whom does this Gospel refer to as "the disciple whom Jesus loved"?

2. John has 21 chapters. True or false?

3. Where did Jesus turn water to wine: Shechem in Samaria, Cana in Galilee, Jerusalem in Benjamin, or Damascus in Syria?

4. Jesus washes the disciples' feet in John 12. True or false?

5. The crucifixion is recounted in John 19. True or false?

6. Who was raised from the dead in John 11?

7. Who were this man's two sisters?

8. What chapter of John includes Jesus' high priestly prayer: 14, 17, 20, or 24?

9. Nicodemus is mentioned in John's Gospel alone. True or false?

10. "Jesus did many other things as well. If every one of them were written down, I suppose that even the whole world would not have room for the books that would be written." This is the last verse of John. True or false?

# Answers to Bible Quiz 64: The Gospel of John

1. Whom does this Gospel refer to as "the disciple whom Jesus loved"?
   **John**

2. John has 21 chapters.
   **True**

3. Where did Jesus turn water to wine: Shechem in Samaria, Cana in Galilee, Jerusalem in Benjamin, or Damascus in Syria?
   **Cana in Galilee**

4. Jesus washes the disciples' feet in John 12.
   **False**

5. The crucifixion is recounted in John 19.
   **True**

6. Who was raised from the dead in John 11?
   **Lazarus**

7. Who were this man's two sisters?
   **Mary and Martha**

8. What chapter of John includes Jesus' high priestly prayer: 14, 17, 20, or 24?
   **17**

9. Nicodemus is mentioned in John's Gospel alone.
   **True**

10. "Jesus did many other things as well. If every one of them were written down, I suppose that even the whole world would not have room for the books that would be written." This is the last verse of John.
    **True**

# Bible Quiz 65: Acts

1. Which book of the Bible is Acts: fifth, forty-third, forty-fourth, or fifty-second?

2. Acts covers only one generation of church history. True or false?

3. The book of Acts ends with Paul's execution during the reign of Nero. True or false?

4. Peter's execution was scheduled to take place in Acts 12. True or false?

5. James' execution took place in Acts 14. True or false?

6. Who was Paul's traveling companion in Acts: Levi, Luke, Clement, or Elmo?

7. In chapter 15, a council convened to consider whether Gentiles must become Jews before becoming Christians. Where did this council take place?

8. Whom did Paul circumcise in chapter 16?

9. In which city is the Areopagus, where Paul preached in chapter 17?

10. What book comes after Acts?

# Answers to Bible Quiz 65: Acts

1. Which book of the Bible is Acts: fifth, forty-third, forty-fourth, or fifty-second?

   **Forty-fourth**

2. Acts covers only one generation of church history.

   **True**

3. The book of Acts ends with Paul's execution during the reign of Nero.

   **False**

4. Peter's execution was scheduled to take place in Acts 12.

   **True**

5. James' execution took place in Acts 14.

   **False**

6. Who was Paul's traveling companion in Acts: Levi, Luke, Clement, or Elmo?

   **Luke**

7. In chapter 15, a council convened to consider whether Gentiles must become Jews before becoming Christians. Where did this council take place?

   **Jerusalem**

8. Whom did Paul circumcise in chapter 16?   **Timothy**

9. In which city is the Areopagus, where Paul preached in chapter 17?

   **Athens**

10. What book comes after Acts?   **Romans**

# Bible Quiz 66: Romans

1. This famous epistle was written to disciples in which city?

2. Had the writer visited the city previously?

3. Who was the writer?

4. What verse contains the theme of the book: 1:17; 2:12; 3:23; or 14:1?

5. How many chapters does Romans have?

6. The letter comes immediately between Acts and 1 Corinthians. True or false?

7. Chapters 9–11 are concerned with the salvation of what group(s): Jews, Gentiles, Samaritans, or all three?

8. Some people think Romans 4 (which teaches justification by faith) directly contradicts James chapter _____ (which seems to teach justification by works).

9. Baptism is described as death, burial, and resurrection with Christ in which chapter: 5, 6, 8, or 13?

10. Romans 14 discusses judgment. True or false?

# Answers to Bible Quiz 66: Romans

1. This famous epistle was written to disciples in which city?

   **Rome**

2. Had the writer visited the city previously?

   **No**

3. Who was the writer?

   **Paul**

4. What verse contains the theme of the book: 1:17; 2:12; 3:23; or 14:1?

   **1:17**

5. How many chapters does Romans have?

   **16**

6. The letter comes immediately between Acts and 1 Corinthians.

   **True**

7. Chapters 9–11 are concerned with the salvation of what group(s): Jews, Gentiles, Samaritans, or all three?

   **The Jews**

8. Some people think Romans 4 (which teaches justification by faith) directly contradicts James chapter _____ (which seems to teach justification by works).

   **2**

9. Baptism is described as death, burial, and resurrection with Christ in which chapter: 5, 6, 8, or 13?

   **6**

10. Romans 14 discusses judging others.

    **True**

# Bible Quiz 67: 1 and 2 Corinthians

1. In which chapter do we find the famous Ode to Love?

2. In which chapter does Paul tell us that he was under such pressure in Asia that he felt the sentence of death?

3. How many chapters are in these two letters combined: 21, 25, 29, or 33?

4. Where is Corinth located: Italy, Greece, Syria, or Cyprus?

5. What chapter in 1 Corinthians includes the extended discussion of the Lord's Supper?

6. What chapters of 2 Corinthians include the extended discussion of the relief offering for poor Christians?

7. Which book comes after 2 Corinthians?

8. Paul mentions his "thorn in the flesh" in 1 Corinthians 12. True or false?

9. In 2 Corinthians 7, Paul says that singles with the gift of celibacy ought to remain unmarried. True or false?

10. Paul established the Corinthian church in Acts 10. True or false?

# Answers to Bible Quiz 67: 1 and 2 Corinthians

1. In which chapter do we find the famous Ode to Love?  **13**

2. In which chapter does Paul tell us that he was under such pressure in Asia that he felt the sentence of death?
   **2 Corinthians 1**

3. How many chapters are in these two letters combined: 21, 25, 29, or 33?
   **29**

4. Where is Corinth located: Italy, Greece, Syria, or Cyprus?  **Greece**

5. What chapter in 1 Corinthians includes the extended discussion of the Lord's Supper?
   **11**

6. What chapters of 2 Corinthians include the extended discussion of the relief offering for poor Christians?
   **8–9**

7. Which book comes after 2 Corinthians?  **Galatians**

8. Paul mentions his "thorn in the flesh" in 1 Corinthians 12.
   **False. It is in 2 Corinthians 12.**

9. In 2 Corinthians 7, Paul says that singles with the gift of celibacy ought to remain unmarried.
   **False. That is found in 1 Corinthians 7.**

10. Paul established the Corinthian church in Acts 10.
    **False. Acts 18 is the correct chapter.**

# Bible Quiz 68: Galatians and Ephesians

1. Who wrote these two letters?

2. Galatians and Ephesians have the same number of chapters. How many?

3. The image of the church as the bride of Christ is found in Galatians. True or false?

4. The statement, "He gave some to be apostles, some to be prophets..." is found in Ephesians. True or false?

5. The famous exhortation to put on the full armor of God is found in Galatians. True or false?

6. "I am astonished that you are so quickly abandoning the one who called you." This is found in Ephesians 1. True or false?

7. The yoke of slavery to the law is mentioned in Galatians 5. True or false?

8. "Awake, O sleeper! Rise from the dead, and Christ will shine on you." This is thought by most scholars to be a baptismal hymn. It is found in Ephesians 5. True or false?

9. Which book follows Ephesians?

10. "From now on let no one cause me trouble, for I bear the marks [stigmata] of Jesus on my body." This is found at the end of Galatians. True or false?

# Answers to Bible Quiz 68: Galatians and Ephesians

1. Who wrote these two letters?   **Paul**

2. Galatians and Ephesians have the same number of chapters. How many?   **Six**

3. The image of the church as the bride of Christ is found in Galatians.
   **False. It is in Ephesians 5.**

4. The statement, "He gave some to be apostles, some to be prophets…" is found in Ephesians.
   **True**

5. The famous exhortation to put on the full armor of God is found in Galatians.
   **False. It is in Ephesians 6.**

6. "I am astonished that you are so quickly abandoning the one who called you." This is found in Ephesians 1.
   **False. It is in Galatians 1.**

7. The yoke of slavery to the law is mentioned in Galatians 5.   **True**

8. "Awake, O sleeper! Rise from the dead, and Christ will shine on you." This is thought by most scholars to be a baptismal hymn. It is found in Ephesians 5.   **True**

9. Which book follows Ephesians?   **Philippians**

10. "From now on let no one cause me trouble, for I bear the marks [stigmata] of Jesus on my body." This is found at the end of Galatians.   **True**

# Bible Quiz 69: Philippians and Colossians

1. These two letters each contain the same number of chapters. How many?

2. Who wrote these letters?

3. Both letters were directed to European churches. True or false?

4. Which of these is a major theme of Philippians: suffering, joy, prophecy, or the millennium?

5. Which of these is a major theme of Colossians: the church, the Holy Grail, circumcision, or spiritual gifts?

6. Which book follows Colossians?

7. Where was the author when he penned these two letters: the Jerusalem temple, a Roman prison, the Hierapolis Hilton, or Arabia?

8. "Let the word of Christ dwell in you richly." This appears in Philippians 3:16. True or false?

9. Philippians 1:21 reads, "For to me, to live is Christ, and to die is gain." True or false?

10. "Be wise in the way you act towards outsiders." This exhortation appears in Colossians 4. True or false?

# Answers to Bible Quiz 69: Philippians and Colossians

1. These two letters each contain the same number of chapters. How many?  **Four**

2. Who wrote these letters?  **Paul**

3. Both letters were directed to European churches.

   **False. Colosse is in Asia.**

4. Which of these is a major theme of Philippians: suffering, joy, prophecy, or the millennium?  **Joy**

5. Which of these is a major theme of Colossians: the church, the Holy Grail, circumcision, or spiritual gifts?

   **The church**

6. Which book follows Colossians?  **1 Thessalonians**

7. Where was the author when he penned these two letters: the Jerusalem temple, a Roman prison, the Hierapolis Hilton, or Arabia?

   **A Roman prison**

8. "Let the word of Christ dwell in you richly." This appears in Philippians 3:16.

   **False. It is in Colossians 3:16.**

9. Philippians 1:21 reads, "For to me, to live is Christ, and to die is gain."

   **True**

10. "Be wise in the way you act towards outsiders." This exhortation appears in Colossians 4.

    **True**

# Bible Quiz 70: 1 and 2 Thessalonians

1. Who wrote these two letters: Paul, Silas, Timothy, or all of these?

2. How many chapters are in these two letters combined: 5, 8, 10, or 15?

3. The "man of lawlessness" is mentioned in 1 Thessalonians. True or false?

4. The idle are to be warned in which chapter: 1 Thessalonians 5, 2 Thessalonians 3, both passages, or neither passage?

5. Thessalonica is in what modern-day country: Italy, Greece, Turkey, or none of these?

6. No one can accurately (or should try to) predict the end of the world, according to 1 Thessalonians 5. True or false?

7. Which book follows 2 Thessalonians?

8. In which chapter of Acts is the Thessalonian church established: 15, 17, 19, or 21?

9. Which chapter of 1 Thessalonians calls us to sexual purity: 3, 4, 5, or 6?

10. "We were delighted to share with you not only the gospel of God, but our lives as well." This appears in which verse?

    - 1 Thessalonians 2:8
    - 2 Thessalonians 1:8
    - 1 Thessalonians 5:12
    - 2 Thessalonians 5:12

# Answers to Bible Quiz 70: 1 and 2 Thessalonians

1. Who wrote these two letters: Paul, Silas, Timothy, or all of these?
   **All of these**

2. How many chapters are in these two letters combined: five, eight, ten, or fifteen?
   **Eight**

3. The "man of lawlessness" is mentioned in 1 Thessalonians.
   **False**

4. The idle are to be warned in which chapter: 1 Thessalonians 5, 2 Thessalonians 3, both passages, or neither passage?
   **Both passages**

5. Thessalonica is in what modern-day country: Italy, Greece, Turkey, or none of these?
   **Greece**

6. No one can accurately (or should try to) predict the end of the world, according to 1 Thessalonians 5.
   **True**

7. Which book follows 2 Thessalonians?   **1 Timothy**

8. In which chapter of Acts is the Thessalonian church established: 15, 17, 19, or 21?   **17**

9. Which chapter of 1 Thessalonians calls us to sexual purity: 3, 4, 5, or 6?   **4**

10. "We were delighted to share with you not only the gospel of God, but our lives as well." This appears in which verse?
    **1 Thessalonians 2:8**

# Bible Quiz 71: 1 and 2 Timothy

1. Who wrote these two letters?

2. To whom were they written?

3. Which of the two letters is longer?

4. To what city was 1 Timothy sent?

5. What was Timothy's mother's name?

6. In which chapter of Acts was Timothy recruited for the mission?

7. "Watch your life and doctrine closely." This appears in which chapter of 1 Timothy: 3, 4, 5, or 6?

8. "Do your best to present yourself to God as one approved." This appears in which chapter of 2 Timothy: 1, 2, 3, or 4?

9. Which book follows 2 Timothy?

10. "Be strong in the grace that is in Christ Jesus." This appears in what chapter: 1 Timothy 2, 2 Timothy 2, 2 Timothy 5, or none of these?

# Answers to Bible Quiz 71: 1 and 2 Timothy

1. Who wrote these two letters?

   **Paul**

2. To whom were they written?

   **Timothy**

3. Which of the two letters is longer?

   **1 Timothy**

4. To what city was 1 Timothy sent?

   **Ephesus**

5. What was Timothy's mother's name?

   **Eunice**

6. In which chapter of Acts was Timothy recruited for the mission?

   **16**

7. "Watch your life and doctrine closely." This appears in which chapter of 1 Timothy: 3, 4, 5, or 6?

   **4**

8. "Do your best to present yourself to God as one approved." This appears in which chapter of 2 Timothy: 1, 2, 3, or 4?

   **2**

9. Which book follows 2 Timothy?

   **Titus**

10. "Be strong in the grace that is in Christ Jesus." This appears in what chapter: 1 Timothy 2, 2 Timothy 2, 2 Timothy 5, or none of these?

    **2 Timothy 2**

# Bible Quiz 72: Titus and Philemon

1. Where was Titus ministering when Paul wrote to him?

2. Paul asked Titus to appoint _____ in every city.

3. Philemon was a runaway slave. True or false?

4. Philemon has only one chapter. True or false?

5. What chapter of Titus includes instructions for dealing with the divisive man: 1, 2, 3, or 4?

6. What chapter includes instructions for silencing false teachers: 1, 2, 3, or 4.

7. What chapter includes specific directions for older men, older women, younger men, and younger women: 1, 2, 3, or 4?

8. Which book follows Philemon in most New Testaments?

9. Who was Onesimus?

10. Where was Paul when he wrote Philemon?

# Answers to Bible Quiz 72: Titus and Philemon

1. Where was Titus ministering when Paul wrote to him?
   **The island of Crete**

2. Paul asked Titus to appoint _____ in every city.
   **Elders**

3. Philemon was a runaway slave.
   **False**

4. Philemon has only one chapter.
   **True**

5. What chapter of Titus includes instructions for dealing with the divisive man: 1, 2, 3, or 4?
   **3**

6. What chapter includes instructions for silencing false teachers: 1, 2, 3, or 4.
   **1**

7. What chapter includes specific directions for older men, older women, younger men, and younger women: 1, 2, 3, or 4?
   **2**

8. Which book follows Philemon in most New Testaments?
   **Hebrews**

9. Who was Onesimus?
   **Philemon's runaway slave**

10. Where was Paul when he wrote Philemon?
    **In prison in Rome**

# Bible Quiz 73: Hebrews

1. Who wrote Hebrews?

2. This letter has 13 chapters. True or false?

3. This letter stresses the superiority of which of these?
   - the Hebrew language
   - Jews over Gentiles
   - Christ
   - the intellectual over the emotional

4. "The word of God is living and active." This is found in which verse: 3:12; 4:12; 5:12; or 6:12?

5. "Encourage one another." This is found in which verse: 3:12; 4:12; 5:12; or 6:12?

6. "We do not want you to become lazy." This is found in which verse: 3:12; 4:12; 5:12; or 6:12?

7. "By now you ought to be teachers." This is found in which verse: 3:12; 4:12; 5:12; or 6:12?

8. Jesus is a high priest, in the order of whom: Methuselah, Mephibosheth, Melchizedek, or Mephistopheles?

9. "And without faith it is impossible to please God." This is found in what verse: 10:6; 11:6; 12:6; or 13:6?

10. Which letter follows Hebrews?

# Answers to Bible Quiz 73: Hebrews

1. Who wrote Hebrews?

   **No one knows for sure.**

2. This letter has 13 chapters.

   **True**

3. This letter stresses the superiority of which of these?

   **Christ**

4. "The word of God is living and active." This is found in which verse: 3:12; 4:12; 5:12; or 6:12?

   **4:12**

5. "Encourage one another." This is found in which verse: 3:12; 4:12; 5:12; or 6:12?

   **3:12**

6. "We do not want you to become lazy." This is found in which verse: 3:12; 4:12; 5:12; or 6:12?

   **6:12**

7. "By now you ought to be teachers." This is found in which verse: 3:12; 4:12; 5:12; or 6:12?

   **5:12**

8. Jesus is a high priest, in the order of whom: Methuselah, Mephibosheth, Melchizedek, or Mephistopheles?

   **Melchizedek**

9. "And without faith it is impossible to please God." This is found in what verse: 10:6; 11:6; 12:6; or 13:6?

   **11:6**

10. Which letter follows Hebrews?

    **James (in most Bibles)**

# Bible Quiz 74: James

1. Who was James?

   the brother of John

   the brother of Jesus

   an apostle and one of the 12

   all the preceding

2. How many chapters are in James: three, five, seven, or nine?

3. Which book follows James?

4. How did James appear most prominently in the book of Acts?

   He stood by while Stephen was martyred (Acts 8).

   He presided over the Jerusalem council (Acts 15).

   He healed the lame man (Acts 3).

   He told Paul, "Your great learning is driving you insane" (Acts 26).

5. Which chapter of James mentions orphans?

6. Which chapter mentions confessing our sins to one another?

7. James 3:6 warns, "The _____ also is a fire, a world of evil among the parts of the body. It corrupts the whole person, sets the whole course of his life on fire, and is itself set on fire by hell."

8. Which chapter warns businesspeople not to put their trust in business and business plans?

9. James 2:26 reads, "As the body without the spirit is dead, so _____ without _____ is dead."

10. James was executed in Jerusalem about AD 62. True or false?

## Answers to Bible Quiz 74: James

1. Who was James?

   **The brother of Jesus**

2. How many chapters are in James: three, five, seven, or nine?

   **Five**

3. Which book follows James?

   **1 Peter**

4. How did James appear most prominently in the book of Acts?

   **He presided over the Jerusalem council (Acts 15).**

5. Which chapter of James mentions orphans?

   **1**

6. Which chapter mentions confessing our sins to one another?

   **5**

7. James 3:6 warns, "The _____ also is a fire, a world of evil among the parts of the body. It corrupts the whole person, sets the whole course of his life on fire, and is itself set on fire by hell."

   **Tongue**

8. Which chapter warns businesspeople not to put their trust in business and business plans?

   **4**

9. James 2:26 reads, "As the body without the spirit is dead, so _____ without _____ is dead."

   **Faith...deeds**

10. James was executed in Jerusalem about AD 62.

    **True**

# Bible Quiz 75: 1 and 2 Peter

1. Who wrote these two letters?

2. How many chapters are in 1 and 2 Peter combined?

3. Which of the two employs more colorful language?

4. What set of three letters follows 1 and 2 Peter?

5. Second Peter 2 warns of false prophets. True or false?

6. First Peter 3 boldly states that baptism saves us. True or false?

7. Second Peter 1 warns of the need to repent before the coming of the Lord. True or false?

8. First Peter 2 calls us to walk in Christ's footsteps and to be willing to suffer. True or false?

9. In 2 Peter 1, the apostle speaks of his imminent death. True or false?

10. Peter was executed in AD 64. Who was the emperor that year?

# Answers to Bible Quiz 75: 1 and 2 Peter

1. Who wrote these two letters?

   **Peter**

2. How many chapters are in 1 and 2 Peter combined?

   **Eight**

3. Which of the two employs more colorful language?

   **2 Peter**

4. What set of three letters follows 1 and 2 Peter?

   **1, 2, and 3 John**

5. Second Peter 2 warns of false prophets.

   **True**

6. First Peter 3 boldly states that baptism saves us.

   **True**

7. Second Peter 1 warns of the need to repent before the coming of the Lord.

   **False**

8. First Peter 2 calls us to walk in Christ's footsteps and to be willing to suffer.

   **True**

9. In 2 Peter 1, the apostle speaks of his imminent death.

   **True**

10. Peter was executed in AD 64. Who was the emperor that year?

    **Nero**

# Bible Quiz 76: 1, 2, and 3 John

1. The apostle John is traditionally thought to be the author of these three letters. True or false?

2. Which of these three letters have only one chapter?

*For questions 3–8, identify the letter in which each quotation or name appears.*

3. "the deceiver and the antichrist"

4. Diotrephes and Demetrius

5. "The elect lady" and "your chosen sister"

6. "Do not love the world."

7. Gaius

8. "Test the spirits."

9. Which book follows 3 John?

10. Which other two New Testament documents have the same general style and themes as 1, 2, and 3 John?

## Answers to Bible Quiz 76: 1, 2, and 3 John

1. The apostle John is traditionally thought to be the author of these three letters.
   **True**

2. Which of these three letters have only one chapter?
   **2 and 3 John**

3. "the deceiver and the antichrist"
   **2 John**

4. Diotrephes and Demetrius
   **3 John**

5. "The elect lady" and "your chosen sister"
   **2 John**

6. "Do not love the world."
   **1 John**

7. Gaius
   **3 John**

8. "Test the spirits."
   **1 John**

9. Which book follows 3 John?
   **Jude**

10. Which other two New Testament documents have the same general style and themes as 1, 2, and 3 John?
    **The Gospel of John and the book of Revelation**

# Bible Quiz 77: Jude and Revelation

1. Who was Jude: the brother of Jesus, an apostle, one of the Beatles, or all of these?

2. How many chapters are in Revelation: 16, 22, 31, or 44?

3. What is the other name for the book of Revelation: the Apocrypha, the Scary Bible Book, the Apostrophe, or the Apocalypse?

4. What positions in the Bible do Jude and Revelation occupy: 63–64, 65–66, 67–68, or 69–70?

*For questions 5–8, identify the letter
in which each phrase appears.*

5. "wild waves of the sea"

6. "the great white throne"

7. "the faith once for all delivered to the saints"

8. "neither hot nor cold"

9. How many churches does Jesus address in Revelation 2–3?

10. What (or whom) does Revelation allude to or quote hundreds of times: Greco-Roman writers, the Old Testament, the four Gospels, or Plato and Aristotle?

# Answers to Bible Quiz 77: Jude and Revelation

1. Who was Jude: the brother of Jesus, an apostle, one of the Beatles, or all of these?

   **The brother of Jesus**

2. How many chapters are in Revelation: 16, 22, 31, or 44?

   **22**

3. What is the other name for the book of Revelation: the Apocrypha, the Scary Bible Book, the Apostrophe, or the Apocalypse?

   **The Apocalypse**

4. What positions in the Bible do Jude and Revelation occupy: 63–64, 65–66, 67–68, or 69–70?

   **65–66**

5. "wild waves of the sea"

   **Jude**

6. "the great white throne"

   **Revelation**

7. "the faith once for all delivered to the saints"

   **Jude**

8. "neither hot nor cold"

   **Revelation**

9. How many churches does Jesus address in Revelation 2–3?

   **Seven**

10. What (or whom) does Revelation allude to or quote hundreds of times: Greco-Roman writers, the Old Testament, the four Gospels, or Plato and Aristotle?

    **The Old Testament**

# 4

# Chronology:
# The Bible, Jesus' Life,
# and Israel's Kings

## Bible Quiz 78: Old Testament Chronology

*Place the following Old Testament events in chronological order.*

1. King David rules Israel.

2. Esther speaks up and saves her people.

3. Solomon answers questions for the Queen of Sheba.

4. Moses receives the Law at Sinai.

5. Joseph is sold into slavery.

6. Joshua fights the battle of Jericho.

# Answers to Bible Quiz 78: Old Testament Chronology

5. Joseph is sold into slavery (around 1900 BC).

4. Moses receives the Law at Sinai (around 1450 BC).

6. Joshua fights the battle of Jericho (around 1400 BC).

1. King David rules Israel (around 1000 BC).

3. Solomon answers questions for the Queen of Sheba (around 950 BC).

2. Esther speaks up and saves her people (around 450 BC).

## Bible Quiz 79: New Testament Chronology

*Place the following New Testament events in chronological order.*

1. Jesus rises from the dead.

2. Paul is executed.

3. First Thessalonians is written.

4. John the Baptist challenges Herod on his sexual immorality.

5. Elizabeth becomes pregnant.

6. Paul is shipwrecked on Malta.

7. Cornelius is baptized.

# Answers to Bible Quiz 79: New Testament Chronology

5. Elizabeth becomes pregnant (6 BC).

4. John the Baptist challenges Herod on his sexual immorality (AD 27).

1. Jesus rises from the dead (AD 30).

7. Cornelius is baptized (AD 40).

3. First Thessalonians is written (AD 50).

6. Paul is shipwrecked on Malta (AD 58).

2. Paul is executed (between AD 65 and 68).

# Bible Quiz 80: Chronology of Jesus' Life, Part 1

*Place the following events from Jesus' life in chronological order.*

1. the Great Commission

2. walking on water

3. the ascension at Bethany

4. circumcision

5. Peter's confession at Caesarea Philippi

6. the appearance to Thomas

7. the trial before Herod

# Answers to Bible Quiz 80: Chronology of Jesus' Life, Part 1

4. circumcision

2. walking on water

5. Peter's confession at Caesarea Philippi

7. the trial before Herod

6. the appearance to Thomas

1. the Great Commission

3. the ascension at Bethany

# Bible Quiz 81: Chronology of Jesus' Life, Part 2

*Place the following events from Jesus' life in chronological order.*

1. ascension

2. Incarnation

3. resurrection

4. parousia (return)

5. baptism

6. transfiguration

7. crucifixion

# Answers to Bible Quiz 81: Chronology of Jesus' Life, Part 2

2. Incarnation

5. baptism

6. transfiguration

7. crucifixion

3. resurrection

1. ascension

4. parousia (return)

# Bible Quiz 82:
## Chronology of the Kings of Israel

*Place the following kings in chronological order.*

1. Manasseh

2. Solomon

3. Josiah

4. David

5. Saul

6. Rehoboam

7. Zedekiah

# Answers to Bible Quiz 82:
## Chronology of the Kings of Israel

5. Saul

4. David

2. Solomon

6. Rehoboam

1. Manasseh

3. Josiah

7. Zedekiah

# About the Bible

## Bible Quiz 83: Translation of the Bible

1. What is a Bible translation?

2. What is a transliteration?

3. Which world language has the greatest number of Bible versions?

4. What is a Bible paraphrase?

5. Arrange the following in order of date of translation.

- Revised Standard Version
- Tyndale
- Holman Christian Standard Bible
- New International Version
- King James Version

## Answers to Bible Quiz 83: Translation of the Bible

1. What is a Bible translation?

    A word-for-word or thought-for-thought rendering of the original Hebrew or Aramaic (Old Testament) or Greek (New Testament) into another language

2. What is a transliteration?

    The transcription of a word from its original language into the letters of another language. For example, *diakonos* (servant) became *deacon*; *baptisma* (immersion) became *baptism*.

3. Which world language has the greatest number of Bible versions?

    English, by far (more than 100 versions)

4. What is a Bible paraphrase?

    A free rendering of the thought of a biblical book according to the understanding of the paraphraser. This is not a translation. The Message by Eugene Peterson is a popular example.

5. Arrange the following in order of date of translation.

    - Tyndale (1500s)

    - King James Version (1600s)

    - Revised Standard Version (completed 1952)

    - New International Version (completed 1978)

    - Holman Christian Standard Bible (completed 1999)

# Bible Quiz 84: Literary Genres of the Bible

*Match the biblical book with its literary genre.*

| | |
|---|---|
| Leviticus | epistle |
| 1 Samuel | narrative |
| Proverbs | prophecy |
| Amos | apocalypse |
| Mark | law |
| Jude | wisdom literature |
| Revelation | Gospel |

## Answers to Bible Quiz 84: Literary Genres of the Bible

Leviticus—law

1 Samuel—narrative

Proverbs—wisdom literature

Amos—prophecy

Mark—Gospel

Jude—epistle

Revelation—apocalyptic

# Bible Quiz 85: Authors of the Bible

*Match the biblical book with its author. Some books were written by more than one person, so in some cases, the correct answer will be the dominant or most eminent writer.*

| | |
|---|---|
| Ecclesiastes | David |
| Numbers | Paul |
| Acts | Micah |
| Titus | John |
| Psalms | Moses |
| Micah | Solomon |
| Revelation | Luke |

## Answers to Bible Quiz 85: Authors of the Bible

Ecclesiastes—Solomon

Numbers—Moses

Acts—Luke

Titus—Paul

Psalms—David

Micah—Micah

Revelation—John

# Bible Quiz 86: Numbers of the Bible

*Match the following numbers with the words
in the second column to which they relate.*

| | |
|---|---|
| 144,000 | Exodus |
| 153 | Matthew–Revelation |
| 603,550 | John |
| 666 | man and the beast |
| 1 | Revelation |
| 260 | Judges |
| 1100 | throughout the Bible |

# Answers to Bible Quiz 86: Numbers of the Bible

144,000—Revelation. This is the symbolic number of the redeemed in heaven (Revelation 7; 14).

153—John. This is the number of fish the disciples hauled ashore (John 21).

603,550—Exodus. This is the number of Israelite soldiers (Exodus 38; Numbers 1).

666—Man and the beast (Revelation 13).

1—Throughout the Bible. It appears more than 2700 times!

260—Matthew–Revelation. This is the number of chapters in the New Testament.

1100—Judges. This is the number of pieces of silver (Judges 16; 17).

# Bible Quiz 87: Cities of the Bible

1. Which famous city was controlled by the Jebusites before David's army took possession of it?

2. How many Antiochs are mentioned in the New Testament?

3. How many Caesareas are mentioned in the New Testament?

4. What was the population of Ai, the second-largest city in Canaan before the Israelites took the Promised Land: 2000, 12,000, 120,000, or 1,200,000?

5. Which Old Testament city had a population of 120,000: Nineveh, Jerusalem, Jericho, or Babylon?

6. With a population of one million, what was the largest city of the Roman Empire: Jerusalem, Athens, Rome, or Alexandria?

7. King Jeroboam of Israel (who lived in the tenth century BC) established centers for false worship in Dan and what other city: Bethel, Bethlehem, Beth Shemesh, or Bethuel?

8. Approximately how many times does the word *city* appear in the Bible: 8, 80, 800, or 8000?

9. How many cities of refuge were allocated for protection from avengers of blood in ancient Israelite times: 2, 6, 66, or 144?

10. Jerusalem was (and is) in the north of Israel. True or false?

# Answers to Bible Quiz 87: Cities of the Bible

1. Which famous city was controlled by the Jebusites before David's army took possession of it?  **Jerusalem**

2. How many Antiochs are mentioned in the New Testament?
   **Two—one in Syria and one in Pisidia**

3. How many Caesareas are mentioned in the New Testament?
   **Two—Caesarea Maritima and Caesarea Philippi**

4. What was the population of Ai, the second-largest city in Canaan before the Israelites took the Promised Land: 2000, 12,000, 120,000, or 1,200,000?
   **12,000 (Joshua 8:25)**

5. Which Old Testament city had a population of 120,000: Nineveh, Jerusalem, Jericho, or Babylon?
   **Nineveh (Jonah 4:11)**

6. With a population of one million, what was the largest city of the Roman Empire: Jerusalem, Athens, Rome, or Alexandria?
   **Rome**

7. King Jeroboam of Israel (who lived in the tenth century BC) established centers for false worship in Dan and what other city: Bethel, Bethlehem, Beth Shemesh, or Bethuel?  **Bethel**

8. Approximately how many times does the word *city* appear in the Bible: 8, 80, 800, or 8000?  **800**

9. How many cities of refuge were allocated for protection from avengers of blood in ancient Israelite times: 2, 6, 66, or 144?  **6**

10. Jerusalem was (and is) in the north of Israel.
    **False**

# Bible Quiz 88: The Land of the Bible, Part 1

1. Which country is *not* mentioned in the Bible: Edom, India, China, or Libya?

2. In which country did Jesus, Joseph, Moses, and Jeroboam all reside at one time or another?

3. The Dead Sea is larger than the Sea of Galilee. True or false?

4. The Dead Sea and the Sea of Galilee are both fresh water bodies. True or false?

5. What is the name for the southern desert of Israel?

6. Place the following cities in order from north to south: Jerusalem, Dan, and Shechem.

7. It never snows in Israel. True or false?

8. What was the western boundary of the Promised Land?

9. Place the following cities in order from east to west: Jericho, Jerusalem, and Gaza.

10. Figs, olives, and grapes all grow in Israel. True or false?

# Answers to Bible Quiz 88: The Land of the Bible, Part 1

1. Which country is *not* mentioned in the Bible: Edom, India, China, or Libya?

   **China**

2. In which country did Jesus, Joseph, Moses, and Jeroboam all reside at one time or another?

   **Egypt**

3. The Dead Sea is larger than the Sea of Galilee.

   **True**

4. The Dead Sea and the Sea of Galilee are both fresh water bodies.

   **False**

5. What is the name for the southern desert of Israel?

   **The Negev**

6. Place the following cities in order from north to south: Jerusalem, Dan, and Shechem.

   **Dan, Shechem, and Jerusalem**

7. It never snows in Israel.

   **False**

8. What was the western boundary of the Promised Land?

   **The Mediterranean Sea**

9. Place the following cities in order from east to west: Jericho, Jerusalem, and Gaza.

   **Jericho, Jerusalem, and Gaza**

10. Figs, olives, and grapes all grow in Israel.

    **True**

# Bible Quiz 89: The Land of the Bible, Part 2

1. *Israel* was the covenant name of which of the patriarchs of Genesis?

2. The word *Palestine* comes from the word for Philistine. True or false?

3. Today, the Jordan River forms part of the border between Israel and Jordan. True or false?

4. The cities of Canaan that the book of Joshua says were burned to the ground were Ai and _____ (in the south) and Hazor (in the north).

5. What was the population of Ai at the time of its destruction: 12,000, 120,000, 1,200,000, or 12,000,000?

6. The tabernacle of the Lord was at Shiloh before it was in Jerusalem. True or false?

7. David reigned 33 years in Jerusalem after reigning approximately 7.5 years in _____.

8. Where did most of the Philistines settle?

   - the coastal plain
   - the hill country
   - the Jordan Valley
   - Transjordan

9. Place these kingdoms in order from east to west: Egypt, Babylonia, and Israel.

10. Technically speaking, the Canaanites lived in Canaan. True or false?

# Answers to Bible Quiz 89: The Land of the Bible, Part 2

1. *Israel* was the covenant name of which of the patriarchs of Genesis?
   **Jacob**

2. The word *Palestine* comes from the word for Philistine.
   **True**

3. Today, the Jordan River forms part of the border between Israel and Jordan.
   **True**

4. The cities of Canaan that the book of Joshua says were burned to the ground were Ai and _____ (in the south) and Hazor (in the north). **Jericho**

5. What was the population of Ai at the time of its destruction: 12,000, 120,000, 1,200,000, or 12,000,000? **12,000**

6. The tabernacle of the Lord was at Shiloh before it was in Jerusalem.
   **True**

7. David reigned 33 years in Jerusalem after reigning approximately 7.5 years in _____.
   **Hebron**

8. Where did most of the Philistines settle? **The coastal plain**

9. Place these kingdoms in order from east to west: Egypt, Babylonia, and Israel. **Babylonia, Israel, and Egypt**

10. Technically speaking, the Canaanites lived in Canaan.
    **True**

# Bible Quiz 90: Brothers of the Bible

1. Who was Simon Peter's brother?

2. Who was Abel's unloving brother?

3. What two brothers were apostles and were dubbed "Sons of Thunder" by Jesus?

4. Jesus had four brothers (Matthew 13). Name them!

5. Who was the father of the brothers Joseph, Benjamin, and Gad?

6. Jesus is called our brother in the New Testament. True or false?

# Answers to Bible Quiz 90: Brothers of the Bible

1. Who was Simon Peter's brother?

   **Andrew**

2. Who was Abel's unloving brother?

   **Cain**

3. What two brothers were apostles and were dubbed "Sons of Thunder" by Jesus?

   **James and John**

4. Jesus had four brothers (Matthew 13). Name them!

   **James, Joseph, Simon, and Judas**

5. Who was the father of the brothers Joseph, Benjamin, and Gad?

   **Jacob (Israel)**

6. Jesus is called our brother in the New Testament.

   **True (Hebrews 2:11)**

# Animals of the Bible

## Bible Quiz 91: Land Animals of the Bible

1. To which two animals does Jesus refer in Matthew 7:6?

2. In Old Testament Law, what animal was allowed as an alternative to a lamb for the Passover meal?

3. Which kind of animal did Jesus ride on in his triumphal entry, in which he fulfilled the prophecy of Zechariah 9:9?

4. What is the connection between the camel and the pig in the Torah?

5. "Don't muzzle the _____ while it is treading out the grain."

6. Are tigers found anywhere in the Bible? How about unicorns?

7. Which animal is mentioned in Song of Songs 2 and again (in reference to Herod) in Luke 13?

8. In Numbers, we meet a talking donkey. Whom was she addressing?

9. Second Peter 2 warns of the perils of being drawn back into the world. Which animals are used as illustrations?

10. A coney is a small, shy, furry mammal that is mentioned a number of times in the Old Testament. What are its other names?

# Answers to Bible Quiz 91: Land Animals of the Bible

1. To which two animals does Jesus refer in Matthew 7:6?
   **Dogs and pigs**

2. In Old Testament Law, what animal was allowed as an alternative to a lamb for the Passover meal?
   **A goat**

3. Which kind of animal did Jesus ride on in his triumphal entry, in which he fulfilled the prophecy of Zechariah 9:9?
   **A donkey**

4. What is the connection between the camel and the pig in the Torah?
   **Both are unclean.**

5. "Don't muzzle the _____ while it is treading out the grain."
   **Ox**

6. Are tigers found anywhere in the Bible? How about unicorns?
   **No, but unicorns do appear in the King James Version.**

7. Which animal is mentioned in Song of Songs 2 and again (in reference to Herod) in Luke 13?
   **Fox**

8. In Numbers, we meet a talking donkey. Whom was she addressing?
   **Balaam**

9. Second Peter 2 warns of the perils of being drawn back into the world. Which animals are used as illustrations?
   **Dogs and pigs (again!)**

10. A coney is a small, shy, furry mammal that is mentioned a number of times in the Old Testament. What are its other names?
    **Hyrax and rock badger**

# Bible Quiz 92: Sea Animals of the Bible

1. What do the eel and the lobster have in common?

2. The end of the book of Job poetically depicts which animal?

3. How many species of saltwater fish inhabit the Sea of Galilee?

4. Who cooks fish for breakfast in John 21?

5. How large was the catch in John 21 after Peter and crew followed the Master's advice?

6. The Bible explicitly states that Jonah was swallowed by a whale. True or false?

7. Which aquatic mammal gave its skin for the furnishings of the tabernacle?

8. What unusual item was once found in a fish's mouth in Matthew 17?

9. What is the biblical name for various (larger) sea creatures?

10. The flood wiped out all fish. True or false?

# Answers to Bible Quiz 92: Sea Animals of the Bible

1. What do the eel and the lobster have in common?
   **Both are unclean.**

2. The end of the book of Job poetically depicts which animal?
   **The crocodile**

3. How many species of saltwater fish inhabit the Sea of Galilee?
   **None. The Sea of Galilee is a freshwater lake.**

4. Who cooks fish for breakfast in John 21?
   **Jesus**

5. How large was the catch in John 21 after Peter and crew followed the Master's advice?
   **153 fish**

6. The Bible explicitly states that Jonah was swallowed by a whale.
   **False. It was a "great fish" according to the NIV.**

7. Which aquatic mammal gave its skin for the furnishings of the tabernacle?
   **Sea cow or manatee**

8. What unusual item was once found in a fish's mouth in Matthew 17?
   **A coin**

9. What is the biblical name for various (larger) sea creatures?
   **Leviathan**

10. The flood wiped out all fish.
    **False**

# Bible Quiz 93: Air Animals of the Bible

1. What sort of bird fed the prophet Elijah in the book of 1 Kings?

2. What do the following have in common: seagull, owl, and bat?

3. According to Jesus, which bird does not fall to the ground apart from our Father's knowledge?

4. "Where the dead body is found, there the _____ will gather."

5. Jesus compares himself to a mother hen. True or false?

6. Who released a dove and a raven?

7. God created birds on which day in Genesis 1?

8. Approximately how many times does the word *bird(s)* appear in the Bible?

9. The phoenix is found in the Bible. True or false?

10. The peacock is found in the Bible. True or false?

# Answers to Bible Quiz 93: Air Animals of the Bible

1. What sort of bird fed the prophet Elijah in the book of 1 Kings?

   **A raven**

2. What do the following have in common: seagull, owl, and bat?

   **They are unclean.**

3. According to Jesus, which bird does not fall to the ground apart from our Father's knowledge?

   **A sparrow**

4. "Where the dead body is found, there the _____ will gather."

   **Vultures**

5. Jesus compares himself to a mother hen.

   **True (Matthew 23:37; Luke 13:34)**

6. Who released a dove and a raven?

   **Noah**

7. God created birds on which day in Genesis 1?

   **Day five**

8. Approximately how many times does the word *bird(s)* appear in the Bible?

   **140 times in the NASB**

9. The phoenix is found in the Bible.

   **False**

10. The peacock is found in the Bible.

    **True (1 Kings 10:22; 2 Chronicles 9:21)**

# Kings of the Bible, Roman Leaders, and King David

## Bible Quiz 94: The Kings of Israel

1. Who was the first king of Israel?

2. Who was his successor?

3. Under whose kingship was Israel formally split into two kingdoms? (Hint: His name begins with an *R*.)

4. Israel (the northern kingdom) was taken into captivity in the eighth century BC. Which foreign power did this: Egypt, Assyria, Babylon, or Persia?

5. Which king was married to Jezebel?

6. Which king of Israel fired only three arrows of victory out of a window in the presence of Elisha?

7. Who was the first king to preside over Israel (the northern kingdom) after the split?

8. Who was the third king of Israel before the split?

9. Approximately how many wives and concubines did this man have?

10. Which Israelite king reigned only seven days?

# Answers to Bible Quiz 94: The Kings of Israel

1. Who was the first king of Israel?

   **Saul**

2. Who was his successor?

   **David**

3. Under whose kingship was Israel formally split into two kingdoms? (Hint: His name begins with an *R*.)

   **Rehoboam**

4. Israel (the northern kingdom) was taken into captivity in the eighth century BC. Which foreign power did this: Egypt, Assyria, Babylon, or Persia?

   **Assyria**

5. Which king was married to Jezebel?

   **Ahab**

6. Which king of Israel fired only three arrows of victory out of a window in the presence of Elisha?

   **Joash**

7. Who was the first king to preside over Israel (the northern kingdom) after the split?

   **Jeroboam I**

8. Who was the third king of Israel before the split?

   **Solomon**

9. Approximately how many wives and concubines did this man have?

   **1000**

10. Which Israelite king reigned only seven days?

    **Zimri**

# Bible Quiz 95: The Kings of Judah

1. Which was the southern kingdom, Israel or Judah?

2. Who was the first Judean king of the divided kingdom?

3. Under whose reign was the long-lost Book of the Law discovered?

4. Whose prayer and faith repulsed the armies of Assyria in 701 BC?

5. What is the significance of the year 587 BC?

6. Which foreign power had been asserting itself in the ancient Near East since the 600s BC?

7. Who was the final king of Judah?

8. How many kings in all reigned in Jerusalem, starting with Saul: 12, 22, or 32?

9. Which Judean king burned the scroll of Jeremiah in the fire, as recorded in Jeremiah 36?

10. Who reigned for 55 years, committed horrendous atrocities and acts of spiritual infidelity, and then genuinely turned to God at the very end of his life?

# Answers to Bible Quiz 95: The Kings of Judah

1. Which was the southern kingdom, Israel or Judah?

   **Judah**

2. Who was the first Judean king of the divided kingdom?

   **Rehoboam**

3. Under whose reign was the long-lost Book of the Law discovered?

   **Josiah**

4. Whose prayer and faith repulsed the armies of Assyria in 701 BC?

   **Hezekiah**

5. What is the significance of the year 587 BC?

   **That was when Judah fell.**

6. Which foreign power had been asserting itself in the ancient Near East since the 600s BC?

   **Babylon**

7. Who was the final king of Judah?

   **Zedekiah**

8. How many kings in all reigned in Jerusalem, starting with Saul: 12, 22, or 32?

   **22**

9. Which Judean king burned the scroll of Jeremiah in the fire, as recorded in Jeremiah 36?

   **Jehoiakim**

10. Who reigned for 55 years, committed horrendous atrocities and acts of spiritual infidelity, and then genuinely turned to God at the very end of his life?

    **Manasseh**

# Bible Quiz 96: Kings of the Nations

1. In biblical times, what was the king of Egypt called?

2. Properly spell this word if you haven't already done so in question 1!

3. Which Persian king was husband to Esther?

4. Egypt is on which continent?

5. Assyria, Babylon, and Persia were all on which continent?

6. Which Babylonian king seems to have suffered from lycanthropy or some other rare disorder? (He ate grass!)

7. Which nation had kings named Shalmaneser, Tiglath-Pileser, and Sargon?

8. Which nation did Belshazzar rule (apparently as second-in-command to Nabonidus in the sixth century BC)?

9. What is the modern name of the nation whose ancient borders (more or less) were those of Persia?

10. Nahum and Jonah demonstrate God's love for the nations—in this case, the nation of _____.

## Answers to Bible Quiz 96: Kings of the Nations

1. In biblical times, what was the king of Egypt called?

   **pharaoh**

2. Properly spell this word if you haven't already done so in question 1!

   **p-h-a-r-a-o-h**

3. Which Persian king was husband to Esther?

   **Xerxes (Ahasuerus)**

4. Egypt is on which continent?

   **Africa**

5. Assyria, Babylon, and Persia were all on which continent?

   **Asia**

6. Which Babylonian king seems to have suffered from lycanthropy or some other rare disorder? (He ate grass!)

   **Nebuchadnezzar**

7. Which nation had kings named Shalmaneser, Tiglath-Pileser, and Sargon?

   **Assyria**

8. Which nation did Belshazzar rule (apparently as second-in-command to Nabonidus in the sixth century BC)?

   **Babylon**

9. What is the modern name of the nation whose ancient borders (more or less) were those of Persia?

   **Iran**

10. Nahum and Jonah demonstrate God's love for the nations—in this case, the nation of _____.

    **Assyria**

# Bible Quiz 97: Roman Leaders

1. Who was emperor when Jesus Christ was born, according to Luke?

2. Who was governor of Judea when Jesus was crucified?

3. What was the name of the half-Jewish, half-Idumean (Edomite) Roman puppet who ruled in Galilee?

4. When did the armies of General Pompey take over in the Middle East: 363 BC, 63 BC, or AD 23?

5. In the Roman army, what was the title of the officer in charge of 100 men?

6. Can you name one such officer? (Hint: Peter visited one in Acts 10.)

7. What is the word used to describe all emperors of Rome after Julius?

8. Can you think of any modern words or terms deriving from this word?

9. Who was the Roman emperor who presided over the Council of Nicaea in AD 325? (Hint: He delayed his baptism until he was on his deathbed, in case he might sin.)

10. Who was the nastiest and most infamous of the Roman emperors? (Hint: He fiddled while Rome burned.)

# Answers to Bible Quiz 97: Roman Leaders

1. Who was emperor when Jesus Christ was born, according to Luke?
   **Tiberius**

2. Who was governor of Judea when Jesus was crucified?   **Pilate**

3. What was the name of the half-Jewish, half-Idumean (Edomite) Roman puppet who ruled in Galilee?
   **Herod**

4. When did the armies of General Pompey take over in the Middle East: 363 BC, 63 BC, or AD 23?
   **63 BC**

5. In the Roman army, what was the title of the officer in charge of 100 men?
   **Centurion**

6. Can you name one such officer? (Hint: Peter visited one in Acts 10.)
   **Cornelius**

7. What is the word used to describe all emperors of Rome after Julius?
   *Caesar*

8. Can you think of any modern words or terms deriving from this word?
   *Caesar salad*, *czar*, and *kaiser*

9. Who was the Roman emperor who presided over the Council of Nicaea in AD 325? (Hint: He delayed his baptism until he was on his deathbed, in case he might sin.)
   **Constantine**

10. Who was the nastiest and most infamous of the Roman emperors? (Hint: He fiddled while Rome burned.)   **Nero**

# Bible Quiz 98: King David, Part 1

1. David, son of _____, son of _____, son of _____ wife of _____.

2. How many brothers did David have? Name two (more for extra credit).

3. Who were David's wives?

4. Name three of David's sons.

5. Who was Jonathan's lame son? (Hint: 2 Samuel 4:4. Extra points if you spell it correctly!)

6. Before David fought Goliath, he was Saul's armor bearer. True or false?

7. _____ the Edomite told Saul that _____ the priest had helped David, so Saul had the priest's family murdered.

8. What does *Nabal* mean?

9. Who was David's descendant and messianic Son?

10. What was Adullam?

## Answers to Bible Quiz 98: King David, Part 1

1. David, son of _____, son of _____, son of _____wife of _____.

   **Jesse...Obed...Ruth...Boaz**

2. How many brothers did David have? Name two (more for extra credit).

   **Seven, including Eliab, Shammah, and Abinadab**

3. Who were David's wives?

   **Michal, Abigail, Ahinoam, and Bathsheba**

4. Name three of David's sons.

   **Absalom, Amnon, and Solomon**

5. Who was Jonathan's lame son? (Hint: 2 Samuel 4:4. Extra points if you spell it correctly!)

   **Mephibosheth**

6. Before David fought Goliath, he was Saul's armor bearer.

   **True**

7. _____ the Edomite told Saul that _____ the priest had helped David, so Saul had the priest's family murdered.

   **Doeg...Ahimelech**

8. What does *Nabal* mean?

   **Fool**

9. Who was David's descendant and messianic Son?

   **Jesus Christ**

10. What was Adullam?

    **The cave where David met with those who were in debt, distressed, and discontent and became their leader (1 Samuel 22)**

# Bible Quiz 99: King David, Part 2

1. Match the commander to the king:

   David

   Saul

   Abner

   Joab

2. The Amalekites raided the city of _____ and carried off David's family.

3. Who was king of Israel after Saul? (It wasn't David!)

4. Who was Uriah?

5. Who said, "You are the man"?

6. Who was David's daughter who was raped?

7. Who was Ahlthophel? (Hint: 2 Samuel 16:23.)

8. Who cursed David and threw rocks at him?

9. Which son of David tried to steal the throne from him?

10. Which books of the Bible describe the life of David?

# Answers to Bible Quiz 99: King David, Part 2

1. Match the commander to the king:

   **David and Joab, Saul and Abner**

2. The Amalekites raided the city of _____ and carried off David's family.

   **Ziklag**

3. Who was king of Israel after Saul? (It wasn't David!)

   **Ish-Bosheth (2 Samuel 2:8)**

4. Who was Uriah?

   **Bathsheba's husband, whom David had killed**

5. Who said, "You are the man"?

   **Nathan**

6. Who was David's daughter who was raped?

   **Tamar**

7. Who was Ahithophel? (Hint: 2 Samuel 16:23.)

   **Absalom's wise counselor**

8. Who cursed David and threw rocks at him?

   **Shimei**

9. Which son of David tried to steal the throne from him?

   **Absolom**

10. Which books of the Bible describe the life of David?

    **1 and 2 Samuel, 1 Chronicles, and 1 Kings**

*Quiz and answers courtesy of Brett Kreider.*

# Miscellaneous

## Bible Quiz 100: The Long and Short of It

1. Which is the longest chapter in the Bible?

2. Which is the shortest chapter in the Bible?

3. How many verses are in the longest chapter in the Bible?

4. What is the shortest verse in the English New Testament?

5. Who lived the longest life in all of biblical history?

6. Name the five one-chapter books of the Bible. (Hint: One is in the Old Testament, and four are in the New Testament.)

## Answers to Bible Quiz 100: The Long and Short of It

1. Which is the longest chapter in the Bible?
   **Psalm 119**

2. Which is the shortest chapter in the Bible?
   **Psalm 117**

3. How many verses are in the longest chapter in the Bible?
   **176**

4. What is the shortest verse in the English New Testament?
   **"Jesus wept" (John 11:35).**

5. Who lived the longest life in all of biblical history?
   **Methuselah**

6. Name the five one-chapter books of the Bible.
   **Obadiah, Philemon, 2 John, 3 John, Jude**

# Bible Quiz 101: Tall and Short, Big and Small

1. Who was the famous giant of the Bible?

2. How tall was he (approximately): seven feet, eight feet, nine feet, or ten feet?

3. Who killed him?

4. What was the name of the tall brother of the giant slayer?

5. What was the name of the tall Israelite monarch who persecuted the giant slayer?

6. Who was the fat man of the book of Judges?

7. Who slew him?

8. What was the name of the short man who climbed a tree to glimpse Jesus?

9. In which Gospel do we read about his conversion?

10. Who was the shortest man in the Bible? (This is a joke question!)

# Answers to Bible Quiz 101: Tall and Short, Big and Small

1. Who was the famous giant of the Bible?
   **Goliath**

2. How tall was he (approximately): seven feet, eight feet, nine feet, or ten feet?
   **Nine feet**

3. Who killed him?   **David**

4. What was the name of the tall brother of the giant slayer?   **Eliab**

5. What was the name of the tall Israelite monarch who persecuted the giant slayer?
   **Saul**

6. Who was the fat man of the book of Judges?   **Eglon**

7. Who slew him?   **Ehud**

8. What was the name of the short man who climbed a tree to glimpse Jesus?
   **Zacchaeus**

9. In which Gospel do we read about his conversion?
   **Luke (chapter 19)**

10. Who was the shortest man in the Bible? (This is a joke question!)
    **Nehemiah (knee-high-my-a). Or how about Bildad the Shuhite (he was shoe-height)? Or even the Philippian jailer (who slept on his watch)?**

*When calculating your score, if you were stumped
by question 10, give yourself credit!*

# Bible Quiz 102: The Beatitudes

1. How many beatitudes does Matthew 5 record?

2. What is the reward for those who hunger and thirst after righteousness?

3. Which other Gospel has a list of beatitudes?

4. Jesus utters another beatitude in Acts 20. What is it?

5. In Romans 4:7, Paul gives a beatitude (quoting Psalm 32): "Blessed are those whose transgressions _____.

*Which book(s) of the Bible contain(s) the following five beatitudes?*

6. "Blessed is the one who reads the words of this prophecy."

7. "Blessed are the dead who die in the Lord."

8. "Blessed are those who are invited to the wedding supper of the Lamb."

9. "Blessed and holy are those who have part in the first resurrection."

10. "Blessed are those who wash their robes."

## Answers to Bible Quiz 102: The Beatitudes

1. How many beatitudes does Matthew 5 record?

   **Eight, including one double beatitude (the last one)**

2. What is the reward for those who hunger and thirst after righteousness?

   **They will be filled.**

3. Which other Gospel has a list of beatitudes?

   **Luke**

4. Jesus gave another beatitude, and Paul mentioned it in Acts 20. What is it?

   **It is more blessed to give than to receive.**

5. In Romans 4:7, Paul gives a beatitude (quoting Psalm 32): "Blessed are those whose transgressions _____."

   **Are forgiven**


*Which book(s) of the Bible contain(s) the following five beatitudes?*

6. "Blessed is the one who reads the words of this prophecy."

   **Revelation (chapter 1)**

7. "Blessed are the dead who die in the Lord."

   **Revelation (chapter 14)**

8. "Blessed are those who are invited to the wedding supper of the Lamb."

   **Revelation (chapter 19)**

9. "Blessed and holy are those who have part in the first resurrection."

   **Revelation (chapter 20)**

10. "Blessed are those who wash their robes."

    **Revelation (chapter 22).**

# Bible Quiz 103: Babies

1. Which famous baby was thrown into the river?

2. Who found him there and had mercy on him?

3. In which town was the baby Jesus born?

4. Who ordered the slaughter of all baby boys up to the age of two residing in this locale?

5. Who were Jesus' mother and (legal) father?

6. Who is portrayed as a baby in the beginning of Ezekiel 16—kicking about and helpless?

7. Which biblical character was never a baby in the first place?

8. How did Jesus react when people brought babies to him to be blessed by him?

   - He rebuked them.
   - He welcomed them.
   - He delegated the blessing to his disciples.

9. What routinely happened to babies in times of famine in the Old Testament?

10. What were the occupations of Shiphrah and Puah (Exodus 1:15)?

# Answers to Bible Quiz 103: Babies

1. Which famous baby was thrown into the river?

   **Moses**

2. Who found him there and had mercy on him?

   **Pharaoh's daughter**

3. In which town was the baby Jesus born?

   **Bethlehem**

4. Who ordered the slaughter of all baby boys up to the age of two residing in this locale?

   **Herod the Great**

5. Who were Jesus' mother and (legal) father?

   **Mary and Joseph**

6. Who is portrayed as a baby in the beginning of Ezekiel 16—kicking about and helpless?

   **"Unfaithful Jerusalem"**

7. Which biblical character was never a baby in the first place?

   **Adam**

8. How did Jesus react when people brought babies to him to be blessed by him?

   **He welcomed them.**

9. What routinely happened to babies in times of famine in the Old Testament?

   **They were eaten (Leviticus 26:29; Deuteronomy 28:53-57; 2 Kings 6:28; Jeremiah 19:9; Ezekiel 5:10).**

10. What were the occupations of Shiphrah and Puah (Exodus 1:15)?

    **They were midwives.**

# Bible Quiz 104: Human Sacrifice

1. Which pagan god of the Old Testament required human sacrifice?

2. Which nation worshipped this god?

3. By which means were babies to be sacrificed?

4. Which Israelite king sacrificed his own son in this way?

5. Which famous patriarch was (in the end) *not* required to sacrifice his son?

6. What was the name of the son?

7. Which book of the Bible recounts this important episode, in a biblical story full of messianic overtones?

8. In 2 Kings 3, which king, in battle against the Israelites, sacrificed his own son on the city walls?

9. In which chapter of Leviticus are the Israelites commanded not to sacrifice their children: 8, 18, or 28?

10. In which location did the Jews routinely perform their child sacrifices?

# Answers to Bible Quiz 104: Human Sacrifice

1. Which pagan god of the Old Testament required human sacrifice?

   **Molech**

2. Which nation worshipped this god?

   **Ammon**

3. By which means were babies to be sacrificed?

   **They were burned.**

4. Which Israelite king sacrificed his own son in this way?

   **Manasseh**

5. Which famous patriarch was (in the end) *not* required to sacrifice his son?

   **Abraham**

6. What was the name of the son?

   **Isaac**

7. Which book of the Bible recounts this important episode, in a biblical story full of messianic overtones?

   **Genesis**

8. In 2 Kings 3, which king, in battle against the Israelites, sacrificed his own son on the city walls?

   **The king of Moab**

9. In which chapter of Leviticus are the Israelites commanded not to sacrifice their children: 8, 18, or 28?

   **18**

10. In which location did the Jews routinely perform their child sacrifices?

    **The Valley of Ben Hinnom (Jeremiah 32:35)**

# Bible Quiz 105: Four Difficult Questions

1. Who was Isaiah's son with a four-part name? (Literally it means "quick to the plunder, swift to the spoil," or "swift is the booty, speedy is the prey.")

2. Only two birthday celebrations are mentioned in the Bible. Can you name the persons? (Hint: There is one in each Testament.)

3. How many fish did Peter and friends net in John 21?

4. What happened to Sosthenes, the Corinthian synagogue ruler, after he was beaten by the anti-Christian mob (Acts 18:7)?

## Answers to Bible Quiz 105: Four Difficult Questions

1. Who was Isaiah's son with a four-part name?

   **Maher-Shalal-Hash-Baz (Isaiah 8:3)**

2. Only two birthday celebrations are mentioned in the Bible. Can you name the persons?

   **Pharaoh (Genesis 40:20) and Herod (Matthew 14:6)**

3. How many fish did Peter and friends net in John 21?

   **153 (And yes, many have tried to attach a symbolic meaning to this number!)**

4. What happened to Sosthenes, the Corinthian synagogue ruler, after he was beaten by the anti-Christian mob (Acts 18:7)?

   **He became a Christian (1 Corinthians 1:1)!**

# Bible Quiz 106:
## Miscellaneous Miscellaneous Questions

1. The word *Bible* does not appear in the Bible. True or false?

2. The word *church* does not appear in the Bible. True or false?

3. First-century church buildings contained pews. True or false?

4. Which book comes after Ezekiel?

5. Which book follows Philippians?

6. How many chapters are in the four Gospels combined: 59, 89, 99, or 209?

7. In which book do we read about Goliath, the Philistine giant?

8. In which book do we read about Eglon, the "Jabba the Hutt" of the Old Testament?

9. In which book do we read about Zacchaeus, the diminutive tax collector who responded so generously to the gospel?

10. Most of the book of Job is poetry. True or false?

# Answers to Bible Quiz 106:
## Miscellaneous Miscellaneous Questions

1. The word *Bible* does not appear in the Bible.

   **True**

2. The word *church* does not appear in the Bible.

   **False**

3. First-century church buildings contained pews.

   **False**

4. Which book comes after Ezekiel?

   **Daniel**

5. Which book follows Philippians?

   **Colossians**

6. How many chapters are in the four Gospels combined: 59, 89, 99, or 209?

   **89**

7. In which book do we read about Goliath, the Philistine giant?

   **1 Samuel**

8. In which book do we read about Eglon, the "Jabba the Hutt" of the Old Testament?

   **Judges**

9. In which book do we read about Zacchaeus, the diminutive tax collector who responded so generously to the gospel?

   **Luke**

10. Most of the book of Job is poetry.

    **True**

# Bible Quiz 107:
# The Cosmic Bible Quiz

(See if you can complete this
100-question quiz in 40 minutes!)

## Section 1: The Old Testament

### Warm-Up Questions

1. What was the final book of the Hebrew Old Testament?

    A. Malachi    B. Chronicles    C. Psalms

2. How many books were in the Hebrew Old Testament?

    A. 39    B. 22    C. 40

3. How many chapters does Ruth have?

    A. three    B. four    C. five

4. How many years did Methuselah live?

    A. 777    B. 919    C. 969

5. The shortest chapter of the Old Testament is...

    A. Psalm 117    B. Jeremiah 45    C. Lamentations 5

### Verse Identification

6. "He will honor a god of fortresses; a god unknown to his fathers he will honor with gold and silver, with precious stones and costly gifts."

    A. Job 4:17        B. 2 Chronicles 11:17
    C. Daniel 11:38     D. Malachi 5:38

7. "Woe to the city of blood, full of lies, full of plunder, never without victims!"

    A. Ezekiel 40:2   B. Zechariah 2:2

    C. Nahum 3:1   D. Habakkuk 2:7

8. "He draws up the drops of water, which distill as rain to the streams."

    A. Psalm 8:4   B. Job 36:27   C. Amos 4:9   D. Genesis 2:7

9. "With a donkey's jawbone I have made donkeys of them. With a donkey's jawbone I have killed a thousand men."

    A. Judges 15:16   B. 1 Samuel 12:12   C. 2 Samuel 17:32

10. "In the thirtieth year, in the fourth month on the fifth day, while I was among the exiles by the Kebar River, the heavens were opened and I saw visions of God."

    A. Jeremiah 1:1   B. Ezekiel 1:1   C. Daniel 1:1   D. Joel 1:1

## Arrange in Order

11. A. Alexander  B. exile in Babylon  C. the Exodus  D. the conquest

12. A. Abraham  B. Ephraim    C. Joseph    D. Jacob  E. Isaac

13. A. Esther    B. Zephaniah    C. Amos    D. Job

14. A. Gehazi    B. Melchizedek    C. Haggai    D. Jethro

15. A. Assyria    B. Persia    C. Rome    D. Babylon    E. Greece

## Warm-Down Questions

16. The Old Testament was written in which two languages?

    A. Latin and Greek   B. Greek and Hebrew

    C. Hebrew and Aramaic

17. Which book does not contain the lesser used of these two languages?

    A. Genesis   B. Ezra   C. Daniel   D. Job

18. Which of the following terms are virtual synonyms?

    A. Pentateuch   B. Law   C. Torah   D. Books of Moses

19. Which verse exhibits the names of God?
    A. Genesis 33:2   B. Exodus 6:3   C. Leviticus 27:27
    D. Numbers 4:4

20. Which two passages contain the Decalogue, or Ten Commandments?
    A. Exodus 20–21

    B. Deuteronomy 5–6

    C. Exodus 20; Deuteronomy 5

    D. Exodus 20; Deuteronomy 6

21. Which two sons of Aaron were struck down?
    A. Nahu and Abidab      B.Uz and Buz
    C. Kenan and Konan      D. Nadab and Abihu

22. How many censuses are taken in Numbers?
    A. one   B. two   C. three

23. How many chapters are in the Law?
    A. 155   B. 187   C. 205   D. 333

24. In the creation account, which day of preparation is paired theologically with day 5 (the day when we see God's providence)?
    A. day 1   B. day 2   C. day 3   D. day 7

25. About how many years ago did Abram live?
    A. 2000   B. 3000   C. 4000

## Section 2: The New Testament

### Warm-Up Questions
26. Who wrote Acts?
    A. Mark   B. Priscilla   C. Luke   D. Peter

27. How many letters are in the New Testament, excluding Acts and Revelation?

    A. 12    B. 18    C. 20    D. 21    E. 23

28. Where was Paul shipwrecked?

    A. Rome    B. Malta    C. Cyprus    D. Cos

29. The New Testament documents were written…

    A. in the Dark Ages by monks

    B. by Nostradamus and company

    C. in the first century by eyewitnesses

    D. on one of Paul's pilgrimages to India

30. How many chapters are in the four Gospels (combined)?

    A. 89    B. 91    C. 93    D. 99

31. The New Testament was written in…

    A. Latin    B. Greek    C. Sanskrit

32. An example of this language is…

    A. Εν αρχη ην ο λογος

    B. *Et creavit Deus hominem*

    C. *Haben Sie ein Dachshund?*

33. How many chapters are in the book of Hebrews?

    A. 10    B. 12    C. 13    D. 15

34. What was Cornelius's rank?

    A. decurion    B. centurion    C. imperator

35. The oldest surviving New Testament manuscript is located in…

    A. Jerusalem    B. Manchester    C. Cairo    D. Tel Aviv

## The Life of Jesus

36. How old was Jesus when he began his ministry?
    A. 12   B. 20   C. 30   D. 40   E. about 30

37. What does *Jesus* mean?
    A. victory   B. salvation   C. messiah

38. What is the Old Testament (Hebraic) form of *Jesus*?
    A. Jacob   B. Joshua   C. Jehovah   D. Jeshurun

39. In which Gospel do magi visit the child Jesus?
    A. Matthew   B. Mark   C. Luke

40. Who was the "King of the Jews" when Jesus was born?
    A. Nero   B. Herod   C. George III   D. Tutankhamun

41. How many half-brothers did Jesus have?
    A. none   B. two   C. four   D. six

42. Which verse shows us that Jesus never used miraculous powers before his official ministry began?
    A. John 2:11   B. Luke 2:11   C. Mark 2:11   D. Matthew 2:11

43. How many New Testament books contain the literal words of Jesus?
    A. four   B. five   C. six   D. seven   E. eight

44. Into whose hands did Jesus entrust his mother while on the cross?
    A. Zebedee's son   B. Zacchaeus' mother
    C. Herod's step-daughter

45. How many Gospels include the feeding of the 5000?
    A. only one   B. two   C. three   D. all four

46. Which Psalm did Jesus quote from the cross?
    A. Psalm 23   B. Psalm 22   C. Psalm 115   D. Psalm 2

47. Jesus' genealogy is found in...
    A. Matthew 1 and Luke 1
    B. Matthew 1 and Luke 3
    C. Luke 1 and Matthew 3
    D. Luke 3 and Matthew 3

48. Which biography of Jesus is shortest?
    A. Matthew    B. Mark    C. Luke    D. John

49. In which chapter of Matthew did Jesus scold the Pharisees?
    A. 11    B. 21    C. 23    D. 25

50. Jesus appeared to his disciples after his resurrection for a period of how many days?
    A. 8    B. 10    C. 40    D. 50

## Warm-Down Questions

51. Which book prophesies the downfall of the Roman Empire?
    A. Matthew    B. Acts    C. Jude    D. Revelation

52. Which two New Testament books have the most in common?
    A. 1 Thessalonians and Colossians
    B. 1 Peter and 1 John
    C. 2 Peter and Jude
    D. 1 Timothy and Mark

53. Which New Testament book has the fewest Greek words?
    A. 2 John    B. 3 John

54. Which museum contains the Codex Alexandrinus and Sinaiticus?
    A. Vatican    B. British    C. Louvre
    D. Imperial War Museum

55. Which is longer, the New Testament or the Koran?
    A. the New Testament    B. the Koran

# Section 3: Theology

56. Purgatory, though found nowhere in the Bible, is found in the...
    A. pseudepigrapha   B. Apocrypha
    C. Nicene Creed   D. Magna Carta

57. Ecclesiology is the study of the...
    A. martyrs   B. church   C. clergy

58. Soteriology is the study of...
    A. salvation   B. sacred music   C. clergy   D. martyrs

59. The fourth word of the ("fish") acronym ICHTHUS is...
    A. Lord   B. Son   C. Savior   D. devotion

60. All the following English Bibles preceded the 1611 KJV except...
    A. Tyndale   B. Coverdale   C. Confraternity
    D. Broad   E. Matthew

61. The Petrine epistles number...
    A. two   B. three   C. four

62. Which Pauline epistle is not written by Paul?
    A. James   B. Hebrews   C. Titus   D. Galatians

63. How many Pastoral epistles are there?
    A. two   B. three   C. four

64. During the last century, most liberal scholars dated the writing of the New Testament documents to which century?
    A. first   B. second   C. third   D. later

65. Theology is literally the study of...
    A. God   B. religion   C. faith   D. belief   E. church

66. The defense of the Christian faith is known as...
    A. polemics   B. vitriolics   C. apologetics   D. humiletics

67. The monastic movement gathered strength in which century?

    A. first   B. second   C. third   D. twelfth

68. The term *gnosticism* comes from the word for...

    A. mysticism   B. knowledge   C. diagnostics

69. Docetists denied that Jesus had a...

    A. physical body   B. immortal soul   C. navel   D. conscience

70. Which of the following is not a monotheistic religion?

    A. Judaism   B. Islam   C. Hinduism   D. Zoroastrianism

71. Which verse says that Christians are baptized by the Holy Spirit?

    A. Acts 2:5             B. Acts 2:38

    C. 1 Corinthians 12:13   D. Ephesians 4:5

72. Which verse clearly refutes the notion of original sin?

    A. Jeremiah 18:20   B. Ezekiel 18:20

    C. Daniel 18:20     D. Matthew 18:20

73. The word *tetragrammaton* refers to the...

    A. four letters of Paul written in AD 55

    B. four doctrines of heretics after AD 100

    C. divine name

    D. resurrection

74. Sikhism was founded by...

    A. Mahavira   B. Nanak   C. Lao Tse   D. Zoroaster

75. The Apocrypha were added to Catholic Bibles in which council?

    A. Vatican II       B. Trent

    C. Fourth Lateran   D. Constantinople

## Section 4: Bible Trivia

76. Which is the shortest verse in the English Bible?
    A. Luke 17:32    B. John 11:25
    C. John 11:35    D. Revelation 1:1

77. Who irreverently tried to steady the ark of the covenant?
    A. Uzzah    B. Urim    C. Uri

78. Clean animals boarded the ark in...
    A. twos    B. sevens    C. fours    D. April of 3106 BC

79. Who first got drunk in the Bible?
    A. Noah    B. Belshazzar    C. Peter    D. Herod Agrippa I

80. The word *Bible* comes from the Greek word for...
    A. holy    B. book    C. scroll    D. double-edged

81. Approximately how many chapters does the Bible have?
    A. 800    B. 1000    C. 1100    D. 1500    E. 1700

82. Titus ministered on the island of...
    A. Cyprus    B. Crete    C. Cos    D. Rhodes

83. Clement records that after release from a Roman prison, Paul reached...
    A. the "Pillars of Hercules" (Spain)
    B. the Philippine Islands
    C. North America
    D. Umtata, Transkei

84. The Tower of Babel is found in which chapter of Genesis?
    A. 8    B. 11    C. 52    D. 66

85. Diagnosis of leprosy is found in which book of the Law?
    A. Exodus   B. Leviticus   C. Numbers   D. Deuteronomy

86. Daniel was written around...
    A. 800 BC   B. 530 BC   C. 400 BC

87. How tall was Goliath?
    A. nine feet, four inches   B. nine feet, nine inches
    C. ten feet, ten inches

88. What is the last word of the Bible?
    A. *God*   B. *amen*   C. *forever*   D. *quickly*   E. *book*

89. Felix was succeeded by...
    A. Festus   B. Agrippa   C. Porcius   D. Drusilla

90. Haggai's contemporary prophet (in 520 BC) was...
    A. Zephaniah   B. Zechariah   C. Micaiah
    D. Obadiah      E. Jeremiah

91. How many were baptized at Pentecost?
    A. 1500   B. 3000   C. 5000

92. How much of Proverbs did Solomon write?
    A. all   B. most   C. some   D. none

93. Who prophesied between 626 and 587 BC?
    A. Isaiah   B. Jeremiah   C. Ezekiel   D. Daniel

94. Who lived longer?
    A. Abraham   B. Job

95. How many books in the Bible have 28 chapters?
    A. one   B. two   C. four

## Super-Hard Bible Questions

96. Wormwood is found in Jeremiah, Lamentations, Revelation, Proverbs and...

    A. Amos    B. 3 Chronicles    C. Psalms

97. Who is the "anointed" in Isaiah 45:1?

    A. Jesus    B. Cyrus    C. Isaiah    D. Daniel    E. Yahweh

98. "*Waydabber YHWH el-moshe bemidhbar*" is the beginning of which book? (Hint: the word *bemidhbar* means "in the desert.")

    A. Galatians    B. Ephesians    C. Numbers
    D. Lamentations    E. Mark

99. Words formed from *Egypt* occur in the Bible approximately...

    A. 100 times    B. 200 times    C. 400 times
    D. 800 times    E. 1600 times

100. A *hapax*, from the Greek word for *once*, is a word occurring only one time in a document. Which hapax occurs in Romans 16:1?

    A. *Cenchreae*

    B. *envelope*

    C. *commend*

    D. *walnut*

    E. *Phoebe*

    F. *aardvark*

    G. *procrastinate*

    H. *cosmic*

*Congratulations! You have completed the Cosmic Bible Quiz!*

# Answers to the Cosmic Bible Quiz

| | | | | |
|---|---|---|---|---|
| 1. B | 21. D | 41. C | 61. A | 81. C |
| 2. B | 22. B | 42. A | 62. B | 82. B |
| 3. B | 23. B | 43. E | 63. B | 83. A |
| 4. C | 24. B | 44. A | 64. B | 84. B |
| 5. A | 25. C | 45. D | 65. A | 85. B |
| 6. C | 26. C | 46. B | 66. C | 86. B |
| 7. C | 27. D | 47. B | 67. C | 87. A |
| 8. B | 28. B | 48. B | 68. B | 88. B |
| 9. A | 29. C | 49. C | 69. A | 89. A |
| 10. B | 30. A | 50. C | 70. C | 90. B |
| 11. B | 31. B | 51. D | 71. C | 91. B |
| 12. B | 32. A | 52. C | 72. B | 92. B |
| 13. D | 33. C | 53. B | 73. C | 93. B |
| 14. A | 34. B | 54. B | 74. B | 94. B |
| 15. B | 35. B | 55. A | 75. B | 95. B |
| 16. C | 36. E | 56. B | 76. C | 96. A |
| 17. D | 37. B | 57. B | 77. A | 97. B |
| 18. D | 38. B | 58. A | 78. B | 98. C |
| 19. B | 39. A | 59. B | 79. A | 99. D |
| 20. C | 40. B | 60. C | 80. B | 100. E |

## Score

| | |
|---|---|
| 0–40 | Keep studying! |
| 41–60 | Average |
| 61–80 | Very good |
| 91–100 | Excellent |

*How did you do? Most Christians taking the test score around 50 points, though a number of better Bible students have scored in the 90s.*

# Test Your Speed

See how long you take to complete these two quizzes. Each period of history has four Bible questions, moving from easier to harder. You are racing against yourself. Answers will not be supplied for this quiz. Learn by finding your own answers!

## Scoring for each of the two tests:

5–10 minutes: You know your Bible well.

11–15 minutes: Good.

16–20 minutes: Fair.

21 or more minutes: Keep studying!

## Bible Quiz 108: The Old Testament

1. Genesis

    A. What is the last word in Genesis?

    B. Who married Rebekah?

    C. In which chapter does Joseph flee Potiphar's wife?

    D. In which chapter do we read about Judah and Tamar?

2. The Law: Exodus–Deuteronomy

    A. From which country did the Exodus take place? What is the name of the man who ruled this country?

    B. How many chapters are in Exodus, Leviticus, Numbers, and Deuteronomy combined?

    C. In which two chapters do we find the Ten Commandments?

    D. Where do we read of the punishment of Nadab and Abihu?

3. The conquest: Joshua

   A. What does God tell Joshua to do in Joshua 1:8?

   B. In which chapter do we find Rahab?

   C. Who was Achan's father?

   D. Which came first, the southern conquest or the northern conquest?

4. The judges: Judges and Ruth

   A. In which chapter do we first read of Samson?

   B. Who was the last judge in the period of the Judges?

   C. What happened to Adoni-Bezek's big toes?

   D. Where do we find the Song of Deborah?

5. The kings: 1 Samuel–2 Chronicles

   A. Who was the first king of Israel?

   B. Who was the king in whose time Israel split into two kingdoms?

   C. How long did Manasseh reign?

   D. How many chapters are in 1 and 2 Samuel combined?

6. The exile: Ezra–Esther, Daniel

   A. Who adopted Esther?

   B. What was Daniel's (new) Babylonian name?

   C. The first paragraph of Ezra is like the last paragraph of which other book?

   D. The four kingdoms of Daniel 7 are also referred to in which other chapter of Daniel?

7. The Psalms

   A. What does Psalm 150 keep saying over and over?

   B. What is the first chapter of each of the five "books" of Psalms?

C. Which Psalm did Moses write?

D. Which Psalm ends by saying, "The darkness is my closest friend"? (Hint: This psalm is in book 3 of Psalms.)

8. Wisdom literature: Job, Proverbs, Ecclesiastes, Song of Songs

A. Does Job's wife have a name?

B. Which proverb in chapter 16 is identical to Proverbs 14:12?

C. What is the beginning of Ecclesiastes talking about?

D. Who were the two companions of Eliphaz?

9. The prophets: Isaiah–Malachi

A. Which prophetic book has exactly 52 chapters?

B. How many books are included in the minor prophets?

C. Where in the New Testament is the last verse of Isaiah quoted?

D. Which New Testament book makes an allusion to Ezekiel 38?

10. The Old Testament (General)

A. What is the last Old Testament book?

B. What is the shortest Old Testament book?

C. What is the parallel chapter to 2 Samuel 24? (Hint: It is somewhere in the Chronicles.)

D. Which two Old Testament passages contain the greatest commandment and the second greatest?

# Bible Quiz 109: The New Testament

1. The Gospels

   A. Which Gospel contains the Sermon on the Mount?

   B. How many chapters are in Mark?

   C. Which Gospel writer recounts the Emmaus Road incident?

   D. In how many of the Gospels do we find the feeding of the 5000?

2. Acts

   A. Who said, "Repent and be baptized"?

   B. On what island were Paul and company shipwrecked?

   C. Where is Paul at the end of the book of Acts?

   D. Who wrote Acts?

3. Paul's letters

   A. Paul wrote Romans: True or false?

   B. Which is the shortest of Paul's letters?

   C. Galatians 2:11 reads, "I opposed him to his face, because he was in the wrong." Whom is Paul referring to?

   D. Which two letters focus the most on salvation by grace through faith?

4. Hebrews

   A. Does Hebrews indicate its author?

   B. "Without faith, it is impossible to_____."

   C. Which chapter focuses on angels?

   D. Which chapter mentions milk and meat?

5. James

   A. In chapter 1, the Word is compared to a _____. Be

careful not to look into it, walk away, and forget what you see!

B. Which book of the Bible comes immediately after James?

C. Confessing sins is mentioned in the last chapter of James. True or false?

D. Which chapter contains these words: "Let your 'Yes' be yes, and your 'No,' no"?

6. Peter's letters

A. How many letters from Peter are in the New Testament?

B. Which chapter of 1 Peter says bluntly, "Baptism saves you"?

C. In which chapter of 2 Peter does the apostle frankly admit that Paul's letters contain some things that are hard to understand?

D. In which chapter of 1 Peter does the apostle advise wives how to win over their unbelieving husbands?

7. John's letters

A. How many letters of John are in the New Testament?

B. According to 2 John, if anyone denies that Jesus came in the flesh, he is a deceiver and the _____. (Hint: the answer begins with an A.)

C. Which other two New Testament books is John thought to have penned?

D. In which letter do we read of Diotrephes and Demetrius?

8. Jude

A. How many verses does Jude have: 15, 25, 45, or 105?

B. Jude refers to Enoch. True or false?

C. Jude refers to the ancient cities of _____ and
_____.

D. The content of Jude is most similar to which book: 2 Corinthians, 2 Peter, or 2 John?

9. Revelation

A. Revelation contains hundreds of allusions to the
_____.

B. On which island was the author of Revelation exiled?

C. Which chapter tells that the saints overcome by the word
of God and the word of their testimony?

D. What is the alternative name for this book?

10. The New Testament (General)

A. How many books are in the New Testament?

B. The longest and shortest New Testament books are
_____ and _____.

C. How many New Testament books have names that begin with the letter *M*?

D. Arrange the following books in chronological order:
1 Timothy, 1 Thessalonians, 2 Timothy, and Romans.